PRESENTED TO:

_____

FROM:

_____

DATE:

_____

GOD'S LITTLE
LESSONS
FOR TEENS

Honor Books
Tulsa, Oklahoma

God's Little Lessons for Teens
ISBN 1-56292-999-2
Copyright © 2001 by Honor Books
P.O. Box 55388
Tulsa, Oklahoma 74155

ATTITUDE

*[Jesus said]: "Truly I say to you, if you have
faith as a mustard seed, you shall say to
this mountain, 'Move from here to there,'
and it shall move; and nothing shall be
impossible to you."*

Matthew 17:20 NASB

*Faith comes by hearing, and hearing by
the word of God.*

Romans 10:17 NKJV

*The boy's father exclaimed, "I do believe;
help me overcome my unbelief!"*

Mark 9:24

*To have faith is to be sure of the things we hope
for, to be certain of the things we cannot see.*

Hebrews 11:1 TEV

THE ATTITUDE DIET

Several years ago, a man was asked to give a commencement address. After he had given his speech, he sat on the platform watching the graduates receive their college degrees. Suddenly, the entire audience began applauding for a student who had earned a perfect 4.0 grade point average. During the applause, a faculty member seated next to the speaker leaned over and said to him, "She may be Miss Genius, but her attitude stinks."

The speaker later said, "Without even thinking, my hands stopped clapping in mid-air. I couldn't help but think, *How sad.*"

No matter how beautiful, intelligent, talented, or athletic you may be, there's no substitute for a positive, loving attitude toward others! You are the foremost architect of the attitude you project.

Be cognizant of the attitudes you "feed" yourself every day. They are the diet of your mind, just as food is the diet of your body. Don't feed yourself with junk ideas, sour opinions, rotten theology, poisoned feelings, or wilted enthusiasm. Instead, feed yourself with the best and most positive ideas, emotional expressions, and thoughtful opinions you have!

GOD'S Little Lessons for Teens

ATTITUDE

As he thinks in his heart, so is he.

Proverbs 23:7 NKJV

A merry heart doeth good like a medicine:
but a broken spirit drieth the bones.

Proverbs 17:22 KJV

Happy are those who fear the LORD. Yes,
happy are those who delight in doing
what he commands.

Psalm 112:1 NLT

When people are happy, they smile, but when
they are sad, they look depressed.

Proverbs 15:13 TEV

STARVE YOUR ANGER

General Horace Porter once wrote about a conversation he had with General Ulysses S. Grant one evening while they were sitting by a campfire. Porter noted, "General, it seems singular that you should have gone through all the rough and tumble of army service and frontier life and have never been provoked into swearing. I have never heard you utter an oath."

Grant replied, "Well, somehow or other, I never learned to swear. When I was a boy, I seemed to have an aversion to it, and when I became a man, I saw the folly of it. I have always noticed, too, that swearing helps to arouse a man's anger, and when a man flies into a passion, his adversary who keeps cool always gets the better of him. In fact, I could never see the value of swearing. I think it is the case with many people who swear excessively that it is a mere habit . . . they do not mean to be profane; to say the least, it is a great waste of time."

Not only does anger give rise to harsh words, but harsh words feed anger. The seething soul uses up valuable inner energy, leaving far less for the normal healthy functioning of spirit, mind, and body. To rid yourself of feelings of anger and frustration, perhaps the first step is to watch your tongue!

ANGER

An angry man stirs up strife, And a hot-tempered man abounds in transgression.

Proverbs 29:22 NASB

Do not associate with one easily angered, or you may learn his ways and get yourself ensnared.

Proverbs 22:24–25

He that is *slow to anger* is *better than the mighty; and he that ruleth his spirit than he that taketh a city.*

Proverbs 16:32 KJV

If you stay calm, you are wise, but if you have a hot temper, you only show how stupid you are.

Proverbs 14:29 TEV

HAMMERING ON OTHERS

One of the most common expressions used to describe losing your temper is to "fly off the handle." This phrase refers to the head of a hammer coming loose from its handle as the carpenter attempts to use it. Several things can happen as a result:

First, the hammer becomes useless—no longer good for work. When you lose your temper, you often lose your effectiveness. Anything you say may not be taken seriously and is likely to be unproductive.

Second, the hammerhead—twirling out of control—is likely to cause some type of damage to anything in its path. When you lose your temper, you cause damage even if you don't realize it—perhaps physically to people or objects in your way, and nearly always emotionally to those who feel they are the victims of this uncontrolled wrath.

Third, the repair of both the hammer and the resulting damage takes time. When you lose your temper, you may recover quickly, but the victim of a hot temper rarely recovers as quickly.

So, as you can see, losing your temper because you're angry is not the best way to handle conflict in life. Keep your temper today. Nobody else wants it.

GOD'S Little Lessons for Teens

ANGER

Wherefore, my beloved brethren, let every man be swift to hear, slow to speak, slow to wrath: For the wrath of man worketh not the righteousness of God.

James 1:19-20 KJV

A gentle answer turns away wrath, but a harsh word stirs up anger.

Proverbs 15:1

You yourselves are to put off all these: anger, wrath, malice, blasphemy, filthy language out of your mouth.

Colossians 3:8 NKJV

Cease from anger, and forsake wrath: fret not thyself in any wise to do evil.

Psalm 37:8 KJV

TABLE OF CONTENTS

INTRODUCTION

If you are a teenager today, you face a myriad of concerns and pressure points that could not even have been imagined a generation ago. Where do you go for answers in these turbulent times? Yes, you have more options, but you also face much more severe consequences for taking the wrong path. You live in a day when a mistake can cost you your life.

This little book has been designed just for you, to help you answer some of those difficult and confusing questions. It is filled with the wisdom of God's Word combined with short devotionals to illustrate the principles. And it's arranged topically so that you can find what you need as situations and circumstances occur. Its topics run the gamut of life's issues, ranging from dealing with anger and loneliness to fear and peer pressure. It offers sound advice concerning relationships, materialism, and worry.

Let *God's Little Lessons for Teens* keep you on the path to a happy and successful life by helping you to escape the pitfalls, preparing you for new challenges, and inspiring you to new levels of personal growth and happiness. Why hesitate? Start learning life's lessons today.

AWFUL ATTITUDE

Cheryl continually complained that she didn't make enough money, couldn't afford the things she wanted, and, therefore, wasn't ever going to amount to anything. A counselor said to her, "You're throwing your energy away complaining instead of using it to get ahead."

"But you don't understand. The job is the problem, not me," Cheryl countered.

The counselor said, "Your low-paying job may be a problem, and your boss may demand too much, but if you are continually that upset, you are causing yourself more harm than either the job or the boss."

"What can I do?" she asked.

The counselor said, "You can't control your boss or the job, but you can control how you *feel* about them. Change your attitude."

Cheryl took her advice. When she stopped whining about her life, people around her noticed. She got a promotion, and with her new job status, she was more marketable. Within a few months, she was transferred out of the department into a position with even higher pay and a more supportive boss.

Awful is a state of *attitude.* A change in attitude will change the state of things!

GOD'S Little Lessons for Teens

CHARACTER

Who is wise and understanding among you?
Let him show it by his good life, by deeds done
in the humilitiy that comes from wisdom.

James 3:13

Remind the people to be subject to rulers and
authorities, to be obedient, to be ready to
do whatever is good.

Titus 3:1

The righteous will hold to their ways, and
those with clean hands will grow stronger.

Job 17:9

"Whoever can be trusted with very little can also
be trusted with much, and whoever is dishonest
with very little will also be dishonest with much."

Luke 16:10

SMALL BITS MATTER A LOT

Have you ever watched an icicle form on a cold winter day? Did you notice how the dripping water froze, one drop at a time, until the icicle was a foot long, or more? If the water was clean, the icicle remained clear and sparkled brightly in the sun, but if the water was slightly muddy, the icicle looked cloudy, its beauty spoiled.

In just this manner our character is formed. Each thought or feeling adds its influence. Each decision we make, whether about matters great or small, will contribute to our singular identity. The things that we take in to our minds and souls—be they impressions, experiences, visual images, or the words of others—will all help to create our character.

We must remain concerned at all times about the "droplets" that influence us. These small bits of experience shape the stability or instability of our lives. Habits of hate, falsehood, and evil intent will mar us like the muddied icicle, eventually destroying us. But acts that develop habits of love, truth, and goodness silently mold and fashion us into the image of God and give us a firm foundation, building our character like the crystal-clear icicle.

17

COMFORT

Trust in him at all times, O people; pour out your hearts to him, for God is our refuge.

Psalm 62:8

You have turned for me my mourning into dancing; You have put off my sackcloth and clothed me with gladness.

Psalm 30:11 NKJV

[Jesus said]: "Therefore you too now have sorrow; but I will see you again, and your heart will rejoice, and no one takes your joy away from you."

John 16:22 NASB

When times are good, be happy; but when times are bad, consider: God has made the one as well as the other.

Ecclesiastes 7:14

COMFORTING RETREAT

Have you ever explored a tidal pool? Low tide is the perfect time to find a myriad of creatures that have temporarily washed ashore from the depths of the sea.

People are often amazed that they can pick up these shelled creatures and stare at them eyeball to eyeball. The creatures rarely exhibit any form of overt fear, such as moving to attack or attempting to scurry away. The creatures simply withdraw into their shells, instinctively knowing they are safe as long as they remain in their strong, cozy shelters.

Likewise, we are safe when we remain in Christ. We are protected from the hassles of life and the fear of unknowns. Those things will come against us, much like the fingers of a brave and curious child trying to invade the sea creature's shell, but they have no power to harm us when we retreat into the shelter of Christ.

The Lord commanded us to learn to *abide* in Him and to *remain* steadfast in our faith. He tells us to *trust* in Him absolutely and to *shelter* ourselves under His strong wings and in the cleft of His rock-like presence. He delights when we *retreat* into His arms for comfort and tender expressions of love.

9

COMFORT

Many are the sorrows of the wicked; But he who trusts in the Lord, lovingkindness shall surround him.

Psalm 32:10 NASB

"Blessed are you who hunger now, for you will be satisfied. Blessed are you who weep now, for you will laugh."

Luke 6:21

The eyes of the Lord are on those who fear him, on those whose hope is in his unfailing love.

Psalm 33:18

You are my hiding place; You shall preserve me from trouble; You shall surround me with songs of deliverance.

Psalm 32:7 NKJV

TALK
TO GOD

One day Lili found herself drowning in a sea of turbulent emotions. She tried to pray and to ask God for help, but she didn't seem to be able to express herself.

Later that day, a friend came by, and Lili began to open up. Soon she was telling her about all the fears, hurts, and struggles she was experiencing. She admitted she was angry with God and disappointed because she felt some of her prayers had not been answered. She felt that she could no longer believe that God was willing to do anything for her.

Finally, as the well of emotion began to subside, Lili's friend said quietly, "I think we just need to talk to God." She placed her arm around Lili's shoulders and prayed a simple, heartfelt prayer. Then she encouraged her with the following words: "God is with you. He always hears our prayers and answers them, though sometimes His answer is not what we would like it to be. Trust Him, and you will see that He always causes things to work out for the best."

No matter what you may be going through today, you can count on God to help you find your way.

GOD'S Little Lessons for Teens

CONFUSION

If you want to know what God wants you to do, ask him, and he will gladly tell you, for he is always ready to give a bountiful supply of wisdom to all who ask him; he will not resent it.

James 1:5 TLB

God is not the author of confusion, but of peace.

1 Corinthians 14:33 KJV

The LORD will accomplish what concerns me; Thy lovingkindness, O LORD, is everlasting.

Psalm 138:8 NASB

Call to Me, and I will answer you, and show you great and mighty things, which you do not know.

Jeremiah 33:3 NKJV

JUST
ONE TREE

A young man was concerned about his future and confused about which direction to take. He sat quietly on a park bench, watching squirrels scamper among the trees. Suddenly, a squirrel jumped from one high tree to another, aiming for a limb so far out of reach that the leap looked like sheer suicide. Though the squirrel missed its mark, it landed safely, and seemingly unconcerned, on a branch several feet below. The squirrel then scampered upward to its original goal, and all was well.

An old man was sitting on the other end of the bench. "Funny thing," he remarked, "I've seen hundreds of 'em jump like that. A lot of 'em miss, but I've never seen any hurt in trying." Then the man chuckled and added, "I guess they've got to risk something if they don't want to spend their lives in just one tree."

The young man thought, *A squirrel takes a chance—don't I have as much nerve as a squirrel?* He made up his mind in that moment to take the risk he had been considering, and sure enough, he landed safer and higher than he had dared to imagine.

Break through confusion by taking a bold leap of faith!

GOD'S Little Lessons for Teens

CONFUSION

*Trust in the Lord completely; don't ever trust
yourself. In everything you do, put God first,
and he will direct you and crown your efforts
with success.*

Proverbs 3:5-6 TLB

*I will instruct thee and teach thee in the way
which thou shalt go: I will guide thee with
mine eye.*

Psalm 32:8 KJV

Where envy and self-seeking exist, *confusion
and every evil thing are there.*

James 3:16 NKJV

*Your ears will hear a word behind you, "This is
the way, walk in it," whenever you turn to the
right or to the left.*

Isaiah 30:21 NASB

FOLLOWING THE GUIDE

Many years ago when Egyptian troops conquered the region of Nubia, a regiment of soldiers crossed the desert with an Arab guide. Their water rations were limited, and the soldiers were suffering from great thirst. Suddenly, a beautiful lake appeared on the horizon. The soldiers insisted that their guide take them to its banks. The guide knew the desert well and recognized that what they were seeing was just a mirage. He told the soldiers that the lake was not real and refused to lose precious time by wandering from the designated course.

Angry words followed. The soldiers decided they didn't need the guide's advice and parted company from him. Yet as the soldiers moved toward the lake, it receded into the distance. Finally, they recognized that the lake was only burning sand. Raging thirst and horrible despair engulfed them. Without their guide, they were lost and without water. Not one of them survived.

Be sure that what you seek today is, not only within the realm of reality, but even more importantly, that it is part of God's plan for your life. Any other goal is likely to be unworthy of your pursuit and may even be deadly.

25

COURAGE

*Don't be afraid, for I am with you. Do not be
dismayed, for I am your God. I will strengthen
you. I will help you. I will uphold you with my
victorious right hand.*

Isaiah 41:10 NLT

*Be strong, and let your heart take courage,
All you who hope in the LORD.*

Psalm 31:24 NASB

*Be on your guard; stand firm in the faith;
be men of courage; be strong.*

1 Corinthians 16:13

*The fear of man brings a snare, But whoever
trusts in the LORD shall be safe.*

Proverbs 29:25 NKJV

THE BRAVEST MAN

Napoleon called Marshall Ney the bravest man he had ever known. Yet Ney's knees trembled so badly one morning before a battle, he had difficulty mounting his horse. When he was finally in the saddle, he shouted contemptuously down at his limbs, "Shake away, knees. You would shake worse than that if you knew where I am going to take you."

Courage is not a matter of being unafraid. It is a matter of taking action even when you are afraid!

Courage is more than sheer bravado shouting, "I can do this!" and launching out with a "do-or-die" attitude over some reckless dare.

True courage is manifest when you choose to take a difficult or even dangerous course of action simply because it is the right thing to do. Courage is looking beyond yourself to what is best for another person.

The source of all courage is God. He promises to stay with you, helping you to accomplish whatever you have determined you must do. No matter what challenge you may be facing in life, God is there to strengthen you and give you the advantage of His infinite wisdom.

27

COURAGE

If we are thrown into the blazing furnace, the God we serve is able to save us from it, and he will rescue us from your hand, O king. But even if he does not, we want you to know, O king, that we will not serve your gods or worship the image of gold you have set up.

Daniel 3:17-18

Don't get tired of helping others. You will be rewarded when the time is right, if you don't give up.

Galatians 6:9 CEV

The members of the council were amazed when they saw the boldness of Peter and John, for they could see that they were ordinary men who had had no special training. They also recognized them as men who had been with Jesus.

Acts 4:13 NLT

Wherefore seeing we also are compassed about with so great a cloud of witnesses, let us lay aside every weight, and the sin which doth so easily beset us, and let us run with patience the race that is set before us.

Hebrews 12:1 KJV

THE COURAGE TO RISK

To laugh is to risk appearing the fool.
To weep is to risk appearing sentimental.
To reach out to another is to risk involvement.
To expose your feelings is to risk revealing
    your inner self.
To place your dreams before the crowd is to
    risk loss.
To love is to risk not being loved in return.
To hope is to risk despair.
To try is to risk failure.
To live is to risk dying.
Not to risk is the greatest risk of all.

"The paradox of courage," G.K. Chesterton once wrote, "is that a person must be a little careless of life in order to survive." Today, if you're wondering if you should stick your neck out or keep your mouth shut, remember that the moment you stop fighting for what matters, you begin to die.

DATING

*You are not to keep company with anyone who
claims to be a brother Christian but indulges in
sexual sins, or is greedy, or is a swindler, or
worships idols, or is a drunkard, or abusive.
Don't even eat lunch with such a person.*

1 Corinthians 5:11 TLB

*God wants you to be holy and to stay away
from sexual sins. He wants each of you to
learn to control your own body in a way
that is holy and honorable.*

1 Thessalonians 4:3–4 NCV

*Keep company with the wise and you will
become wise. If you make friends with stupid
people, you will be ruined.*

Proverbs 13:20 TEV

*Walk in the way of good men, And keep
to the paths of the righteous.*

Proverbs 2:20 NASB

CONSISTENT CHARACTER

A boy and his girlfriend found it hard to find time for special dates because of their busy schedules. The boy decided that a casual picnic in the park would be relaxing and fun, so he and his girlfriend went into a fast-food restaurant and ordered a bag of chicken to go. Moments earlier, the manager had placed the day's cash in a plain paper bag and set it at the side of the serving counter. Another clerk reached for the couple's chicken order and mistakenly gave them the bag of money. The couple paid for their order, got in their car, and drove to the park for their picnic. But when they opened the bag, they found that there were no drumsticks, only greenbacks!

After briefly discussing their find, the boy decided the right thing to do was to return the money. When they arrived at the restaurant, the manager was ecstatic. "I can't believe it!" he said. "You've got to be the two most honest people in this city."

Though their special date didn't turn out as planned, the boy's integrity and honesty won his girlfriend's heart. Consistent strength of character is more important than occasional tokens of romance.

31

DATING

*A man who is not married is busy with the
Lord's work, trying to please the Lord. . . .
A woman who is not married or a girl who
has never married is busy with the Lord's work.
She wants to be holy in body and spirit.*
                    1 Corinthians 7:32,34 NCV

Do not stir up nor awaken love Until it pleases.
                    Song of Solomon 2:7 NKJV

*Do not be deceived: "Bad company corrupts
good morals."*
                    1 Corinthians 15:33 NASB

*Do not be yoked together with unbelievers.
For what do righteousness and wickedness
have in common? Or what fellowship can
light have with darkness?*
                    2 Corinthians 6:14

FOCUS ON LIFE

In 1928, a happy, ambitious, young nursing student was diagnosed with tuberculosis. Her family sent her to a sanitarium in Saranac Lake for what they hoped would be only a few months. However, Isabel Smith was unable to leave the sanitarium for twenty-one years.

Many people would have given up, but not Isabel. She never ceased to pursue the art of living. She read voraciously, loved to write letters, and taught other patients to read and write.

While ill, Isabel met a kind gentleman who was also a patient at the sanitarium. They began to date as best they could in their restrictive surroundings. They studied together, read to each other, and kept each other company. Isabel dreamed of marrying him one day and having a little house in the mountains. Finally, after her discharge from the sanitarium, they did marry. She then wrote a book about all the good things life had brought her and earned enough in royalties to buy her mountain retreat.

Isabel Smith was not focused on dating. She was focused on living. That's the key to finding a relationship that will stand the test of time.

33

DEATH AND LOSS

We know that our body—the tent we live in here on earth—will be destroyed. But when that happens, God will have a house for us. . . . it will be a home in heaven that will last forever.

2 Corinthians 5:1 NCV

"Blessed are those who mourn, For they shall be comforted."

Matthew 5:4 NKJV

He died for us so that, whether we are awake or asleep, we may live together with him.

1 Thessalonians 5:10

If the Spirit of God, who raised Jesus from death, lives in you, then he who raised Christ from death will also give life to your mortal bodies by the presence of his Spirit in you.

Romans 8:11 TEV

STRENGTH IN OTHERS

In both fall and spring, geese can be seen migrating in a beautiful V-shaped formation. Scientists have discovered that the lead goose does the most work by breaking the force of the headwinds. At certain intervals, relative to the strength of the headwinds, the lead goose will drop back and take up a position at the end of the formation. A goose next to the former leader will take the lead spot in the "V."

Scientists have calculated that it takes up to 60 percent less effort for geese to fly this way. The flapping of all those wings creates an uplift of air. The uplift effect is greatest at the rear of the formation. In essence, the geese are taking turns "uplifting" one another. After a turn at the point of the "V," the lead goose is allowed to rest and be "carried" by the others until it regains its strength and gradually moves forward in the formation to take its place in the lead role again.

When we face death or loss, we need friends and family around us who can cooperate and work together. All can be "lifted up" when that happens. Is there someone today you can "uplift" with friendship, caring, or prayer?

35

DEATH AND LOSS

*We know that in everything God works for good
with those who love him, who are called
according to his purpose.*

Romans 8:28 RSV

*And I am convinced that nothing can ever
separate us from his love. Death can't, and life
can't. The angels can't, and the demons can't.
Our fears for today, our worries about
tomorrow, and even the powers of hell can't
keep God's love away. Whether we are high
above the sky or in the deepest ocean, nothing
in all creation will ever be able to separate us
from the love of God that is revealed in Christ
Jesus our Lord.*

Romans 8:38-39 NLT

*If we live, we live to the Lord; and if we die, we
die to the Lord. So, whether we live or die, we
belong to the Lord.*

Romans 14:8

*The bodies we now have are weak and can die.
But they will be changed into bodies that are
eternal. Then the Scriptures will come true,
"Death has lost the battle! Where is its victory?
Where is its sting?"*

1 Corinthians 15:54-55 CEV

EVERY EXIT IS AN ENTRANCE

Author-pastor John Claypool offers a reassuring perspective on the experience of loss:

I've learned something through all my experiences—that every exit is also an entrance. Every time you walk out of something, you walk into something. I got into this world by dying in the womb—and it must have been painful to get ripped out of that familiar place—but that was the prerequisite of my getting into time and space. At the end of my life in history there's going to be a similar kind of transition experience. If we can get at the terror of death by saying it is a transformer rather than an annihilator, then perhaps we can get rid of the idea that death is a thief and is taking something that is rightfully ours, which is the basis of all the rage that I know.

Death is the ultimate experience of loss, of course, and it often overshadows all our other losses. You can learn to deal with the fear of death and even the loss of a friend or loved one if you can come to view your loss as a "transformer rather than an annihilator."

DEPRESSION

In my great trouble I cried to the Lord and he answered me; from the depths of death I called, and Lord, you heard me!

Jonah 2:2 TLB

Answer me quickly, O LORD; my spirit fails. Do not hide your face from me or I will be like those who go down to the pit. Let the morning bring me word of your unfailing love, for I have put my trust in you. Show me the way I should go, for to you I lift up my soul.

Psalms 143:7-8

I will refresh the weary and satisfy the faint.

Jeremiah 31:25

The LORD also will be a refuge for the oppressed, A refuge in times of trouble.

Psalm 9:9 NKJV

OVERCOMERS

In 1980, Mount Saint Helens erupted, and the Pacific Northwest shuddered under its devastating impact. Forests were destroyed by fire. Rivers were choked with debris. Fish and other wildlife died. Toxic fumes filled the air, and reporters ominously predicted that acid rain would develop from the ash-laden clouds. The future for the area seemed bleak.

Nevertheless, less than a year after the eruption, scientists discovered that despite the fact that the rivers had been clogged with hot mud, volcanic ash, and floating debris, some of the salmon and steelhead had managed to survive. By using alternate streams and waterways, some of which were less than six inches deep, the fish returned home to spawn.

Within a few short years, the fields, lakes, and rivers surrounding Mount Saint Helens teemed with life. The water and soil seemed to benefit from the nutrients supplied by the exploding volcano. Even the mountain itself began to show signs of new vegetation.

No matter how dismal the outlook may be, don't give up! Challenges in life can enrich you and make you stronger. Remember, you are God's creation, and you were designed to overcome!

DEPRESSION

*We have troubles all around us, but we are
not defeated. We do not know what to do, but
we do not give up the hope of living. We are
persecuted, but God does not leave us. We are
hurt sometimes, but we are not destroyed.*

2 Corinthians 4:8-9 NCV

*Cast your burden upon the L*ORD*, and He will
sustain you; He will never allow the righteous
to be shaken.*

Psalm 55:22 NASB

*G*OD IS OUR *refuge and strength, a tested help
in times of trouble.*

Psalm 46:1 TLB

*[Jesus said]: "In this world you will have trouble.
But take heart! I have overcome the world."*

John 16:33

THE FOG OF DEPRESSION

On a cool morning in July of 1952, Florence Chadwich waded into the waters off Catalina Island, intending to swim the channel to the California coast. Though an experienced long-distance swimmer, Florence knew this swim would be difficult. The water was numbingly cold, and the fog was so thick she could hardly see the boat that carried her trainer.

Florence swam for more than fifteen hours. Several times she could sense sharks swimming next to her in the inky waters. Rifles were fired from the trainer's boat to help keep the sharks at bay. Yet when Florence looked around her, all she could see was the fog. When she finally asked to be lifted from the water, she was only a half-mile from her goal. In a later interview Florence admitted that it wasn't the cold, fear, or exhaustion that caused her to fail in her attempt to swim the Catalina channel. It was the fog.

The struggles we face can sometimes cloak us in a fog of depression. Remember, even if you can't see the end of your trouble, press on. God hasn't brought you this far to leave you. He is standing there just outside the fog, waiting for your call.

D I S C O U R A G E M E N T

My mouth would encourage you; comfort
from my lips would bring you relief.

Job 16:5

You are my hiding place from every storm of life;
you even keep me from getting into trouble!
You surround me with songs of victory.

Psalm 32:7 TLB

Those who know you, LORD, will trust you; you
do not abandon anyone who comes to you.

Psalm 9:10 TEV

When life is good, enjoy it. But when life
is hard, remember: God gives good times
and hard times.

Ecclesiastes 7:14 NCV

YOU MUSTN'T QUIT

When things go wrong, as they sometimes
    will;
When the road you're trudging seems all uphill;
When the funds are low and the debts are high,
And you want to smile, but you have to sigh;
When care is pressing you down a bit—
Rest! If you must—but never quit.
Life is queer, with its twists and turns,
As every one of us sometimes learns.
And many a failure turns about
When he might have won if he'd stuck it out.
Stick to your task, though the pace seems slow.
You may succeed with one more blow.
Success is failure turned inside out,
The silver tint of the clouds of doubt.
And you never can tell how close you are,
It may be near when it seems far.
So stick to the fight when you're hardest hit.
It's when things seem worst that
You mustn't quit!

—Unknown

DISCOURAGEMENT

We gladly suffer, because we know that suffering helps us to endure. And endurance builds character, which gives us a hope that will never disappoint us. All of this happens because God has given us the Holy Spirit, who fills our hearts with his love.

Romans 5:3-5 CEV

[Love] always protects, always trusts, always hopes, always perseveres.

1 Corinthians 13:7

Blessed is the man who endures trial, for when he has stood the test he will receive the crown of life which God has promised to those who love him.

James 1:12 RSV

May the Lord direct your hearts into God's love and Christ's perseverance.

2 Thessalonians 3:5

AN OATH OF PERSEVERANCE

I will never give up so long as I know I'm right.

I will believe that all things will work out for me if I hang on until the end.

I will be courageous and undismayed in the face of odds.

I will not permit anyone to intimidate me or deter me from my goals.

I will fight to overcome all physical limitations and setbacks.

I will try again and again and yet again to accomplish my dreams.

I will take new faith and resolution from the knowledge that all successful people have had to overcome defeat and adversity.

I will never surrender to discouragement or despair, no matter what.

—Herman Sherman

Recite these vows very often. Keep them with you, and review them when you're stuck in a pressure-filled situation, tossing and turning at night, or just plain discouraged.

45

DOUBT

[Jesus said]: "Stop your doubting, and believe!"
John 20:27 TEV

---

*God has said, "I will never, never fail you nor
forsake you."*

Hebrews 13:5 TLB

---

*[Jesus said]: "Truly I say to you, whoever says
to this mountain, 'Be taken up and cast into
the sea,' and does not doubt in his heart, but
believes that what he says is going to happen,
it shall be granted him."*

Mark 11:23 NASB

---

*Why are you downcast, O my soul? Why so
disturbed within me? Put your hope in God,
for I will yet praise him, my Savior and my God.*
Psalm 42:11

ONE IN A HUNDRED

Tommy John was the leading pitcher in the National League in 1974. His team was on its way to the World Series. But during a game in September, Tommy ruptured a ligament in his elbow. When he asked his surgeon if he had any chance of pitching again, he was told, "The odds are one in a hundred."

Shortly after his operation and with his arm in a cast, Tommy and his family went to church. The sermon that morning was about Abraham and Sarah and the child that was born when they were well advanced in years. The minister looked right at Tommy as he said, "You know, with God, nothing is impossible."

That was all Tommy needed to hear. Praying for God's strength, he began the daily work of rehabilitation. His progress was slow, but finally, he was able to bend his little finger to touch his thumb. After eighteen months of this painful process, Tommy John walked back onto the pitcher's mound, eventually pitching more games after his surgery than before.

If you have asked God for a miracle in your life, doubt your doubt and boot it out. You can trust God to help you overcome any situation.

47

DOUBT

The one who doubts is like the surf of the sea driven and tossed by the wind.

James 1:6 NASB

Let us hold firmly to the hope that we have confessed, because we can trust God to do what he promised.

Hebrews 10:23 NCV

[Jesus said]: "If you have faith as a mustard seed, you will say to this mountain, 'Move from here to there,' and it will move; and nothing will be impossible for you."

Matthew 17:20 NKJV

Be merciful to those who doubt; snatch others from the fire and save them.

Jude 1:22–23

DOUBT NOT

On May of 1996, Los Angeles Dodger Brett Butler checked into the hospital for what he thought would be a simple tonsillectomy, but the surgeons found that he had cancer. The news hit Butler hard. His mother had died of cancer a year before. Now he found himself facing the possibility of his own death at the age of thirty-eight.

Butler was stunned at first, but he soon decided to respond with faith rather than doubt. He underwent two operations and thirty-two radiation treatments, determined to return to the Dodgers' lineup. Few believed he could do it, but Butler didn't waver. "I believe God answers prayer," he told his friends and family. "I want to acknowledge that in some capacity. This is an opportunity to show I am a disciple for Christ. Now I'll be able to measure my success from the lowness of my career."

Finally, on September 6, Butler was once again in uniform on the ball field. Because of his faith and persistence, he scored a run and fielded two nice catches to help his team win the game.

Though the events in your life may seem overwhelming, respond in faith instead of doubt, and watch God turn those struggles into opportunities for your success.

DRUGS OR ALCOHOL

Be not drunk with wine, wherein is excess; but be filled with the Spirit.

Ephesians 5:18 KJV

Those who sleep, sleep at night, and those who get drunk, get drunk at night. But since we belong to the day, let us be self-controlled.

1 Thessalonians 5:7–8

The wrong things the sinful self does are clear: . . . feeling envy, being drunk, having wild and wasteful parties, and doing other things like these.

Galatians 5:19,21 NCV

Let us conduct ourselves properly, as people who live in the light of day—no orgies or drunkenness, no immorality or indecency, no fighting or jealousy.

Romans 13:13 TEV

HAVING A BAD DAY

Donnie felt overwhelmed with failure. Alcohol had wreaked havoc on his life, and although he had been alcohol-free for some months and was involved in Alcoholics Anonymous, on this day he could see no future for himself. Finally, desperately discouraged, he decided to visit Chuck, a friend from his AA group.

When Donnie arrived, he found Chuck sitting in his room. They began to talk, and Chuck told him that things weren't going well at school. They spent nearly two hours talking and encouraging each other. On the way home, Donnie thought to himself, *At least I've made it through the day.*

A few days later he saw Chuck again. "Hey, Donnie, thanks," he said. "When you came by the other day, my life seemed hopeless. I was so discouraged that I was thinking about going out and getting drunk. You helped me see that God is still working in my life."

Donnie was surprised to hear Chuck's confession. He thought he was the one who had been helped by their time together.

When you are feeling hopeless and overwhelmed, seek out a friend. Discouragement and temptation always seem more daunting when you're alone. And you may find that God meets your need while He is using you to meet someone else's.

51

DRUGS OR ALCOHOL

Woe to those who rise early in the morning that they may pursue strong drink; Who stay up late in the evening that wine may inflame them! . . . they do not pay attention to the deeds of the LORD, Nor do they consider the work of His hands.

Isaiah 5:11–12 NASB

Don't let the sparkle and the smooth taste of strong wine deceive you. For in the end it bites like a poisonous serpent.

Proverbs 23:31–32 TLB

Wine is a mocker and beer a brawler; whoever is led astray by them is not wise.

Proverbs 20:1

Those who live according to the flesh set their minds on the things of the flesh, but those who live according to the Spirit, the things of the Spirit.

Romans 8:5 NKJV

RIGHT IS ALWAYS RIGHT

Stephen R. Covey once spoke to a large group of college students on the subject of the "new reality." He asserted that there are some principles in this world that should be respected no matter how much you believe in personal freedom.

One student contended that right and wrong are not absolutes, but matters of personal interpretation based on the situation. Not so, Covey argued. Our actions always have consequences. When we do those things we know are wrong, we pay a price. As Covey looked around the room, he could tell that some people believed his arguments were outdated.

Then Covey asked the students to sit quietly for a few moments and ask themselves whether they knew in their hearts what the truth was. At the end of the session, several of the students admitted they weren't quite so sure of themselves anymore. One young man even said that he had changed his mind completely.

God has placed the truth within you. Though you may choose not to listen, your heart will always tell you what is right. When you are tempted to go along with the crowd, stop and listen to God's truth within your heart.

53

FAILURE

I am very happy to brag about my weaknesses.
Then Christ's power can live in me.

2 Corinthians 12:9 NCV

Our High Priest is not one who cannot feel
sympathy for our weaknesses. . . . Let us have
confidence, then, and approach God's throne,
where there is grace. There we will receive
mercy and find grace to help us just when
we need it.

Hebrews 4:15–16 TEV

If we believe not, yet he abideth faithful:
he cannot deny himself.

2 Timothy 2:13 KJV

Plans go wrong for lack of advice; many
counselors bring success.

Proverbs 15:22 NLT

PUSHING PAST FAILURE

Sparky didn't have much going for him. He failed every subject in the eighth grade, and in high school, he flunked Latin, algebra, English, and physics. He made the golf team but promptly lost the most important match of the season and then lost the consolation match. He was also awkward socially. While in high school, he never once asked a girl to go out on a date.

Only one thing was important to Sparky—drawing. He was proud of his artwork even though no one else appreciated it. He submitted cartoons to the editors of his high school yearbook, but they were turned down. Even so, Sparky aspired to be an artist. After high school, he sent samples of his artwork to Walt Disney Studios. Again, he was turned down.

Still, Sparky didn't quit! He decided to write his own autobiography in cartoons. The character he created became famous worldwide—the subject, not only of cartoon strips, but countless books, television shows, and licensing opportunities.

Sparky, you see, was Charles Schulz, creator of the "Peanuts" comic strip. Like his main character, Charlie Brown, Schulz seemed unable to accomplish many things. But, rather than letting rejection stop him, he made the most of what he could do!

GOD'S Little Lessons for Teens

FAILURE

At least there is hope for a tree: If it is cut down, it will sprout again, and its new shoots will not fail. Its roots may grow old in the ground and its stump die in the soil, yet at the scent of water it will bud and put forth shoots like a plant.

Job 14:7-9

And the Lord said, "Simon, Simon, behold, Satan hath desired to have you, that he may sift you as wheat: But I have prayed for thee, that thy faith fail not: and when thou art converted, strengthen thy brethren."

Luke 22:31-32 KJV

We can rejoice, too, when we run into problems and trials, for we know that they are good for us—they help us learn to endure. And endurance develops strength of character in us, and character strengthens our confident expectation of salvation.

Romans 5:3-4 NLT

We never give up. Our bodies are gradually dying, but we ourselves are being made stronger each day.

2 Corinthians 4:16 CEV

TOP TEN FAILURES OF ALL TIME

1. The engineer who neglected to design a reverse gear in the first car he manufactured.
2. The group turned down by Decca Records because "guitars are on their way out."
3. The illustrator told by his newspaper editor to pursue another line of work.
4. The skinny kid who hated the way he looked and was always being beaten up by bullies.
5. The seriously ill, deeply in debt composer who in desperation wrote an oratorio in a few hours.
6. The obese, bald, deformed eccentric who became a reclusive thinker.
7. The orchestra conductor-composer who made his greatest contributions after becoming deaf.
8. The politician who lost his first seven elections.
9. The boy everyone thought was mute because his stutter was so bad he never spoke until he was a teenager.
10. The woman born deaf and blind who became a great writer and philanthropist and once said, "I thank God for my handicaps."

Answers: Henry Ford; The Beatles; Walt Disney; Charles Atlas; George Frederick Handel *(The Messiah);* Socrates; Ludwig von Beethoven; Abraham Lincoln; James Earl Jones; Helen Keller.

Our greatest failures can produce our greatest successes.

57

FAITH

What is faith? It is the confident assurance that what we hope for is going to happen. It is the evidence of things we cannot yet see.

Hebrews 11:1 NLT

Above all, taking the shield of faith, wherewith ye shall be able to quench all the fiery darts of the wicked.

Ephesians 6:16 KJV

We walk by faith, not by sight.

2 Corinthians 5:7 NKJV

"Everything is possible for him who believes."

Mark 9:23

A TUG ON THE LINE

A twelve-year-old boy accepted Jesus Christ as his personal Savior and Lord during a weekend revival meeting. The next week, his school friends questioned him about the experience.

"Did you hear God talk?" one asked.

"No," the boy said.

"Did you have a vision?" another asked.

"No," the boy replied.

"Well, how did you know it was God?" a third friend asked.

The boy thought for a moment and then said, "It's like when you catch a fish. You can't see the fish or hear the fish; you just feel it tugging on your line. I felt God tugging on my heart."

So often we try to figure out life by what we can see, hear, or experience with our other senses. We make calculated estimates and judgments based on empirical evidence. There's a level of truth, however, that cannot be perceived by the senses or measured objectively. It's at that level where faith abounds. It is our faith that compels us to believe, even when we cannot explain to others why or how. By our faith, we only know in whom we trust. And that is sufficient.

FAITH

*When I look at the night sky and see the work
of your fingers—the moon and the stars you
have set in place—what are mortals that you
should think of us, mere humans that you
should care for us? For you made us only
a little lower than God, and you crowned us
with glory and honor.*

Psalms 8:3-5 NLT

*Let love and faithfulness never leave you; bind
them around your neck, write them on the
tablet of your heart.*

Proverbs 3:3

*Every child of God can defeat the world, and our
faith is what gives this victory.*

1 John 5:4 CEV

*"His master said to him, 'Well done, good and
faithful servant; you have been faithful over a
little, I will set you over much; enter into the joy
of your master.'"*

Matthew 25:21 RSV

FRANTIC FAITH

Bruce Larson tells this story about a test of his faith:

A few years ago I almost drowned in a storm at sea in the Gulf of Mexico when I found myself swimming far from shore, having tried to retrieve my drifting boat. The waves were seven or eight feet high, and the sky was dark with gale force winds and lightning. I can remember saying, "Well, this is it."

I was drifting out to sea when the word of the Lord came to me and saved my life. What I thought He said was, "I'm here, Larson, and you're not coming home as soon as you think. Can you tread water?"

Somehow that had never occurred to me. Had I continued my frantic effort to swim back to shore, I would have exhausted my strength and gone down.

Too often we make matters worse by our frantic efforts to save ourselves when God is trying to tell us, "Stand still." We get ourselves into hopeless situations, and the more we do, the worse it gets.

The next time you are faced with a challenge, remember to rest in God. Have faith in His promises, and trust in His unfailing love.

GOD'S Little Lessons for Teens

FAMILY

*He will direct his children and his household
after him to keep the way of the LORD by
doing what is right and just.*

Genesis 18:19

---

*They said, "Believe in the Lord Jesus, and you
shall be saved, you and your household."*

Acts 16:31 NASB

---

*If someone does not know how to lead the
family, how can that person take care of
God's church?*

1 Timothy 3:5 NCV

---

*You must make allowance for each other's
faults and forgive the person who offends you.
Remember, the Lord forgave you, so you
must forgive others.*

Colossians 3:13 NLT

A PICTURE-PERFECT CHRISTMAS

During the Depression, many families could scarcely afford the bare essentials, much less Christmas presents. "But, I'll tell you what we can do," a father said to his six-year-old son, Pete. "We can use our imaginations and make pictures of the presents we would like to give each other."

For the next few days, each member of the family worked secretly, but joyfully. On Christmas morning, huddled around a scraggly tree adorned with a few pitiful decorations, the family gathered to exchange the presents they had created. And what gifts they were! Daddy got a shiny black limousine and a red motor boat. Mom received a diamond bracelet and a new hat. Little Pete had fun opening his gifts, a drawing of a swimming pool and pictures of toys cut from magazines.

Then it was Pete's turn to give his present to his parents. With great delight, he handed them a brightly colored crayon drawing of three people—a man, a woman, and a little boy. They had their arms around one another, and under the picture was one word: US. Even though other Christmases were far more prosperous for this family, no Christmas in the family's memory stands out as more precious than the year they discovered their greatest gift was each other.

63

FAMILY

Choose for yourselves this day whom you will serve. . . . But as for me and my house, we will serve the LORD.

Joshua 24:15 NKJV

Be ye kind one to another, tenderhearted, forgiving one another, even as God for Christ's sake hath forgiven you.

Ephesians 4:32 KJV

Teach a child to choose the right path, and when he is older he will remain upon it.

Proverbs 22:6 TLB

Children, obey your parents in the Lord, for this is right. "Honor your father and mother"— which is the first commandment with a promise—"that it may go well with you and that you may enjoy long life on the earth."

Ephesians 6:1–3

RAISED
IN LOVE

"The family," says Mother Teresa, "is the place to learn Jesus. God has sent the family—together as husband and wife and children—to be His love."

In *Words to Love By,* Mother Teresa writes:

Once a lady came to me in great sorrow and told me that her daughter had lost her husband and a child. All the daughter's hatred had turned on the mother. So I said, "Now you think a bit about the little things that your daughter liked when she was a child. Maybe flowers or a special food. Try to give her some of these things without looking for a return. And she started doing some of these things, like putting the daughter's favorite flower on the table, or leaving a beautiful piece of cloth for her. And she did not look for a return from the daughter. Several days later the daughter said, "Mommy, come. I love you. I want you." By being reminded of the joy of childhood, the daughter reconnected with her family. She must have had a happy childhood to go back to the joy and happiness of her mother's love.

Today, think of some special ways to remind your family of your love for them; then put them into action!

65

FEAR

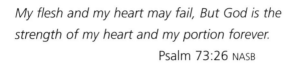

*My flesh and my heart may fail, But God is the
strength of my heart and my portion forever.*

Psalm 73:26 NASB

*In the day of my trouble I will call upon You,
For You will answer me.*

Psalm 86:7 NKJV

*Let us be bold, then, and say, "The Lord is my
helper, I will not be afraid. What can anyone
do to me?"*

Hebrews 13:6 TEV

*God hath not given us the spirit of fear; but
of power, and of love, and of a sound mind.*

2 Timothy 1:7 KJV

FACE YOUR FEAR

In 1993, a deranged fan stabbed tennis star Monica Seles, narrowly missing her spinal cord. She recognized her assailant as a man she had seen loitering around her hotel, but she had no idea why he had attacked her. At the hospital, she couldn't stop thinking, *What if he comes back?* That night, her parents and brother all stayed in her hospital room with her. Monica was assured that her attacker was in custody. Even so, she had flashbacks of his face, the blood-stained knife, and her own screams.

Six months after the attack, her assailant was given two years probation and set free. Her fear intensified, and she sought out a psychologist to help her. Encouraged by her peers, she made a decision to return to tennis. Then came yet another blow. A German judge upheld her assailant's suspended sentence, which had been appealed. She said to herself, *Monica, you have to move on.* Three months later, she played an exhibition match and scored two wins—one on the court, and one in her mind and heart.

Are you facing a fear that seems insurmountable? Be encouraged. The God who never leaves you or forsakes you will be with you, strengthening you every step of the way.

FEAR

God is our refuge and strength, A very present help in trouble. Therefore we will not fear, though the earth should change, And though the mountains slip into the heart of the sea.

Psalms 46:1-2 NASB

My slanderers pursue me all day long; many are attacking me in their pride. When I am afraid, I will trust in you. In God, whose word I praise, in God I trust; I will not be afraid. What can mortal man do to me?

Psalms 56:2-4

That he would grant unto us, that we being delivered out of the hand of our enemies might serve him without fear.

Luke 1:74 KJV

So do not fear, for I am with you; do not be dismayed, for I am your God. I will strengthen you and help you; I will uphold you with my righteous right hand.

Isaiah 41:10

TIGERS IN THE DARK

One night at a circus that drew a packed audience of children and their parents, the tiger trainer came out to perform. After bowing to loud applause, he went into the cage. A hush drifted over the audience as the door was locked behind him.

Suddenly, as the trainer skillfully put the tigers through their paces, everyone heard a loud *Pop!* followed by a complete power failure. For several long minutes the trainer was locked in the dark with the tigers. Though he could not see them, he knew they could see him with their powerful night vision. A whip and a small kitchen chair seemed meager protection.

Finally the lights came back on, and the trainer finished his performance. Later, in a TV interview, he admitted his first chilling fears. Then he realized that the tigers did not know he could not see them. "I just cracked my whip and talked to them," he said, "until the lights came on."

At some point in life everyone will confront the terror of "tigers in the dark." The assurance we have is that with God's help, our terrors never will be able to exploit their temporary advantage over us.

GOD'S Little Lessons for Teens

FORGIVENESS

*Let the wicked leave their way of life and
change their way of thinking. Let them
turn to the LORD, our God; he is merciful
and quick to forgive.*

Isaiah 55:7 TEV

*"Come now, and let us reason together,"
Says the LORD, "Though your sins are as scarlet,
they will be as white as snow; Though they
are red like crimson, They will be like wool."*

Isaiah 1:18 NASB

*Blessed is he whose transgressions are forgiven,
whose sins are covered.*

Psalm 32:1

*Be kind to each other, tenderhearted, forgiving
one another, just as God has forgiven you
because you belong to Christ.*

Ephesians 4:32 TLB

SET FREE

Years after her experience in a Nazi concentration camp, Corrie ten Boom found herself standing face to face with one of the most cruel and heartless German guards she had known while in the camps. This man had humiliated and degraded both her and her sister, jeering at them and visually raping them as they stood in the delousing shower.

Now he stood before her with an outstretched hand, asking, "Will you forgive me?"

Corrie said:

> I stood there with coldness clutching at my heart, but I know that the will can function regardless of the temperature of the heart. I prayed, "Jesus, help me!" Woodenly, mechanically, I thrust my hand into the one stretched out to me, and as I did, I experienced an incredible thing. The current started in my shoulder, raced down into my arm, and sprang into our clutched hands. Then this warm reconciliation seemed to flood my whole being, bringing tears to my eyes. "I forgive you, brother," I cried with my whole heart. For a long moment we grasped each other's hands, the former guard, the former prisoner. I have never known the love of God so intensely as I did in that moment!

When you forgive, you set a prisoner free—yourself!

FORGIVENESS

*If we confess our sins, he is faithful and just
to forgive us our sins, and to cleanse us from
all unrighteousness.*

1 John 1:9 KJV

*You, LORD, are good, and ready to forgive,
and abundant in mercy to all those who call
upon You.*

Psalm 86:5 NKJV

*The LORD declares: "I am the One who forgives
all your sins, for my sake; I will not remember
your sins."*

Isaiah 43:25 NCV

*If my people will humble themselves and pray,
and search for me, and turn from their wicked
ways, I will hear them from heaven and forgive
their sins and heal their land.*

2 Chronicles 7:14 TLB

SHAKE
HANDS

Laura Ingalls Wilder once had an old dog named Shep. As he grew older, Shep's eyesight became poor, and he didn't always recognize friends. Wilder writes, "Once he made a mistake and barked savagely at an old friend whom he really regarded as one of the family, though he had not seen him for some time. Later, as we all sat in the yard, Shep seemed uneasy. At last he walked deliberately to the visitor, sat up, and held out his paw. It was so plainly an apology that our friend said, 'That's all right, Shep, old fellow! Shake and forget it!' Shep shook hands and walked away perfectly satisfied."

Harboring a grudge or remembering a slight or injustice will only bring the hard shell of bitterness to your heart. Yet people are often quicker to judge than they are to forgive. Unresolved bitterness and failure to forgive will, not only destroy relationships, but also elevate your blood pressure, increase your risk of stroke, cause myriad aches and pains, and affect your ability to get a good night's sleep.

Is there an apology you need to make today or an offer of forgiveness you need to extend? Then shake hands, forgive, and forget. You'll be glad you did.

73

FRIENDSHIP

*Two are better than one; because they have a
good reward for their labour. For if they fall,
the one will lift up his fellow.*

Ecclesiastes 4:9-10 KJV

*A friend loves at all times, And a brother
is born for adversity.*

Proverbs 17:17 NASB

*Wounds from a friend are better than many
kisses from an enemy.*

Proverbs 27:6 NLT

*There are friends who pretend to be friends, but
there is a friend who sticks closer than a brother.*

Proverbs 18:24 RSV

WINNING FRIENDS

Dale Carnegie, author of *How To Win Friends and Influence People,* is considered one of the greatest "friend winners" of the century. He taught, "You can make more friends in two months by becoming interested in other people than you can in two years by trying to get other people interested in you."

To illustrate his point, Carnegie would explain that dogs seem to have mastered the fine art of making friends better than most people. When you get within ten feet of a friendly dog, it will begin to wag its tail, a visible sign that it welcomes and enjoys your presence. If you take time to pet the dog, it will become excited, lick you, and jump all over you to show how much it appreciates you. The dog became man's best friend by being genuinely interested in people!

One of the foremost ways in which we show our interest in others is to listen to them—to ask questions, intently listen to their answers, and ask further questions based upon what they say. The person who feels "heard" is likely to seek out this friendly listener again and again and to count that person as a great friend.

75

FRIENDSHIP

"Abraham believed God, and it was credited to him as righteousness," and he was called God's friend.

James 2:23

As iron sharpens iron, so one man sharpens another.

Proverbs 27:17

"The greatest love you can have for your friends is to give your life for them. And you are my friends if you do what I command you."

John 15:13–14 TEV

The sweet smell of perfume and oils is pleasant, and so is good advice from a friend.

Proverbs 27:9 NCV

FRIENDS MAKE FRIENDS

The complex shapes of snowflakes have confounded scientists for centuries. In the past, scientists believed that the making of a snowflake was a two-step process. They believed that inside the winds of a winter storm a microscopic speck of dust would become trapped in a molecule of water vapor. Scientists suggested that this particle would then become heavily frosted with droplets of super-cooled water and plunge to earth. During its descent, the varying temperature and humidity would sculpt the heavy, icy crystal into a lacy snowflake. Or at least that's what scientists used to believe.

In recent decades, the true formation of the snowflake was discovered. Very few snowflakes actually contain dust or other particles. Dr. John Hallett, of the University of Nevada, discovered that the majority of snowflakes are formed from fragments of other snowflakes. As snowflakes are formed, extremely dry or cold air causes them to break up into smaller parts. The small fragments then act as seeds for new snowflakes to develop. Most snow is made, therefore, by snow!

In like manner, friendly people generate friends. Their neighborly outlook inspires others to reach out and be friendly too. Pass along the seed of friendship, and watch what develops in your own life.

FRUSTRATION

*Call to Me, and I will answer you, and show
you great and mighty things, which you do
not know.*

Jeremiah 33:3 NKJV

*We know that all things work together for
good to them that love God, to them who
are the called according to his purpose.*

Romans 8:28 KJV

*Encourage the exhausted, and strengthen the
feeble. Say to those with an anxious heart, "Take
courage, fear not. Behold, your God will come."*

Isaiah 35:3–4 NASB

*God is faithful; he will not let you be tempted
beyond what you can bear. But when you are
tempted, he will also provide a way out so
that you can stand up under it.*

1 Corinthians 10:13

GETTING SOMEWHERE

A frustrated young man once approached a successful businessman. "Success completely eludes me," he said. "I want to get somewhere in life."

"That's great!" the successful man replied. "And exactly where do you want to go?"

The young man's reply was inconclusive. "Well, I don't know for sure. But I'm not happy with the way things are."

The successful man probed, "What can you do best? What skills do you have? What do you think you're cut out for?"

The young man pondered the question and then replied, "I don't believe I have any particular skills. But I think I'm entitled to a better break."

The successful man tried a third time, "All right then. What would you *like* to do if you could have any job you wanted?" The young man's answer was vague and uncertain once again.

Finally the successful man advised, "Young man, you will always be frustrated. If you don't know where you want to go, how will you ever know when you have arrived?"

To alleviate frustration in your life, fix your sight on a specific destination or goal. Sharpen and clarify it. Then, take the necessary steps to begin to move toward your goal, rather than toward a vague "somewhere."

79

FRUSTRATION

The LORD says, "My thoughts are not like your thoughts. Your ways are not like my ways."

Isaiah 55:8 NCV

If God is on our side, who can ever be against us? Since he did not spare even his own Son for us but gave him up for us all, won't he also surely give us everything else?

Romans 8:31–32 TLB

I will make an eternal covenant with them. I will never stop doing good things for them, and I will make them fear me with all their heart, so that they will never turn away from me.

Jeremiah 32:40 TEV

Though I walk in the midst of trouble, You will revive me; You will stretch out Your hand Against the wrath of my enemies, And Your right hand will save me. The LORD will perfect that which concerns me.

Psalms 138:7–8 NKJV

GOING GOD'S WAY

Antonio Salieri, an ambitious, but mediocre eighteenth-century composer offers this prayer in the film *Amadeus:*

Lord, make me a great composer. Let me celebrate Your glory through music. And be celebrated myself. Make me famous throughout the world, dear God, make me immortal. After I die, let people speak my name forever with love for what I wrote. In return I will give You my chastity, my industry, my deep humility, my life.

When it became obvious to the superficially pious Salieri that he would never be as gifted as Wolfgang Amadeus Mozart, his life became fraught with jealousy and frustration. He plotted to destroy Mozart and turned away from God, convinced that God had betrayed him.

When you feel frustrated in an attempt to achieve a goal or position, make sure you are going God's way and following His plan. Legislating how God will use you, even in a great work for Him, will result in frustration rather than the satisfaction found in allowing Him to plan the way, the means, and the use of your life.

GOD'S Little Lessons for Teens

G I V I NG

He who gives to the poor will lack nothing,
but he who closes his eyes to them receives
many curses.

Proverbs 28:27

"Give to everyone who asks you, and if
anyone takes what belongs to you, do
not demand it back."

Luke 6:30

"Give, and it will be given to you. A good
measure, pressed down, shaken together
and running over, will be poured into your
lap. For with the measure you use, it will
be measured to you."

Luke 6:38

Each man should give what he has decided
in his heart to give, not reluctantly or under
compulsion, for God loves a cheerful giver.

2 Corinthians 9:7

HONEYCOMB GIVERS

There are three kinds of givers: the flint, the sponge, and the honeycomb. Which kind are you?

To get anything from the flint, you must hammer it. Yet, all you generally get are chips and sparks. The flint gives nothing away if it can help it, and even then only with a great display.

To get anything from the sponge, you must squeeze it. It readily yields to pressure, and the more it is pressed, the more it gives. Still, you must push.

To get anything from the honeycomb, however, you must only take what freely flows from it. It gives its sweetness generously, dripping on all without pressure, without begging or badgering.

Note, too, that there is another difference in the honeycomb. It is a renewable resource. Unlike the flint or sponge, the honeycomb is connected to life; it is the product of the ongoing work and creative energy of bees.

If you are a "honeycomb giver," your life will be continually replenished as you give. And, as long as you are connected to the Source of all life, you can never run dry. When you give freely, you will receive in like manner, so that whatever you give away will soon be multiplied back to you.

GOD'S Little Lessons for Teens

G I V I N G

God did not keep back his own Son, but he gave him for us. If God did this, won't he freely give us everything else?

Romans 8:32 CEV

If I give all I possess to the poor and surrender my body to the flames, but have not love, I gain nothing.

1 Corinthians 13:3

In everything I did, I showed you that by this kind of hard work we must help the weak, remembering the words the Lord Jesus himself said: "It is more blessed to give than to receive."

Acts 20:35

God has given gifts to each of you from his great variety of spiritual gifts. Manage them well so that God's generosity can flow through you.

1 Peter 4:10 NLT

A GENEROUS SPIRIT

Chad was a shy, quiet little boy. One day he came home and told his parents he wanted to make a valentine for everyone in his class. That night his dad and mom talked about it. Chad wasn't very popular. The other kids didn't include him in their games. He always walked home by himself. What if he went to all the trouble and then didn't receive any valentines?

They decided to encourage him anyway. Chad worked after school for three long weeks. On Valentine's Day, he excitedly put his handiwork into a paper bag and bolted out the door. Trying to be prepared for his disappointment, his parents had plans to take him out for ice cream that night.

After school, Chad came running home—arms empty. His folks expected him to burst into tears. "Not a one, not a one," he kept saying. His parents looked at him with wounded eyes. Then he added, "I didn't forget a single kid!"

One of the beautiful benefits of being generous toward others is that it's so rewarding it changes the way you look at the world.

GOSSIP

A gossip betrays a confidence, but a
trustworthy man keeps a secret.

Proverbs 11:13

Where there is *no wood, the fire goes out;*
And where there is *no talebearer, strife ceases.*

Proverbs 26:20 NKJV

Their words are like an open pit, and their
tongues are good only for telling lies.

Romans 3:13 CEV

Post a guard at my mouth, God, set a watch
at the door of my lips.

Psalm 141:3 THE MESSAGE

THE UNTAMED TONGUE

Many analogies have been given for the "untamed tongue." Quarles likened it to a drawn sword that takes a person prisoner: "A word unspoken is like the sword in the scabbard, thine; if vented, thy sword is in another's hand."

Others have compared evil speaking to the following things:

- A freezing wind—one that seals up the sparkling waters and kills the tender flowers and shoots of growth. In similar fashion, bitter and hate-filled words bind up the hearts of people and cause love to cease to flourish.
- A fox with a firebrand tied to its tail, sent out among the standing corn just as in the days of Samson and the Philistines. So gossip spreads without control or reason.
- A pistol fired in the mountains, the echo of which is intensified until it sounds like thunder.
- A snowball that gathers size as it rolls down a mountain.

Perhaps the greatest analogy, however, is one given by a little child who came running to her mother in tears. "Did your friend hurt you?" the mother asked.

"Yes," said the girl.

"Where?" asked her mother.

"Right here," said the child, pointing to her heart.

Ask God to place a watch over your tongue. Your words have the power to hurt and tear down, but they also have the power to heal and build up.

GOSSIP

The words of gossip are like choice morsels;
they go down to a man's inmost parts.

Proverbs 18:8

They have become filled with every kind of
wickedness, evil, greed and depravity. They are
full of envy, murder, strife, deceit and malice.
They are gossips. . . . those who do such things
deserve death.

Romans 1:29,32

Gossips can't keep secrets, so avoid people
who talk too much.

Proverbs 20:19 NCV

Women must *likewise* be *dignified, not malicious*
gossips, but temperate, faithful in all things.

1 Timothy 3:11 NASB

GOLDEN GOSSIP

Laura Ingalls Wilder writes the following in *Little House in the Ozarks:*

I know a little band of friends that calls itself a woman's club. There is no obligation and there are no promises; but in forming the club and in selecting new members, only those are chosen who are kind-hearted and dependable as well as the possessors of a certain degree of intelligence and a small amount of that genius which is the capacity for careful work. In short, those who are taken into membership are those who will make good friends, and so they are a little band who are each for all and all for each. . . .

They are getting so in the habit of speaking good words that I expect to see them all develop into Golden Gossips.

Ever hear of golden gossip? I read of it some years ago. A woman who was always talking about her friends and neighbors made it her business to talk of them, in fact, never said anything but good of them. She was a gossip, but it was "golden gossip." This woman's club seems to be working in the same way.

Who wouldn't enjoy belonging to such a group! Strive to mold your circle of friends into a Golden Gossip Club.

GOD'S Little Lessons for Teens

GUIDANCE

*Ask the LORD to bless your plans, and you
will be successful in carrying them out.*

Proverbs 16:3 TEV

*The steps of a good man are ordered by
the LORD: and he delighteth in his way.*

Psalm 37:23 KJV

*Yet I am always with you; you hold me by my
right hand. You guide me with your counsel,
and afterward you will take me into glory.*

Psalms 73:23-24

*I will instruct you (says the Lord) and guide
you along the best pathway for your life; I will
advise you and watch your progress.*

Psalm 32:8 TLB

THE GUIDE

While skiing in Colorado one day, a man noticed some people on the slope wearing red vests. Moving closer, he could read these words on their vests: BLIND SKIER. He couldn't believe it. He had difficulty skiing with 20/20 vision! How could people without sight manage to ski?

He watched the skiers for a while and discovered their secret. Each skier had a guide who skied beside, behind, or in front of him or her, always in a position where the two could easily communicate. The guides used two basic forms of communication. First, they would tap their ski poles together to assure the blind skiers that they were there, and second, they would speak simple, specific directions: "Go right. Turn left. Slow. Stop. Skier on your right."

The skier's responsibility was to trust the guide to give good instructions and to immediately and completely obey those instructions.

We can't see even five seconds into the future. We cannot see the struggles to come. Other people may run into us, or we into them, like errant skiers on a crowded slope. But God has given us the Holy Spirit to be our Guide through life—to walk before and behind us and to dwell in us. Our role is to listen and to obey.

GOD'S Little Lessons for Teens

GUIDANCE

This God is our God for ever and ever; he will be our guide even to the end.

Psalm 48:14

The LORD will continually guide you, And satisfy your desire in scorched places, And give strength to your bones; And you will be like a watered garden, And like a spring of water whose waters do not fail.

Isaiah 58:11 NASB

Trust in the LORD with all thine heart; and lean not unto thine own understanding. In all thy ways acknowledge him, and he shall direct thy paths.

Proverbs 3:5–6 KJV

Show me your ways, O LORD, teach me your paths; guide me in your truth and teach me.

Psalms 25:4–5

WATCH WHAT YOU CATCH

A dog once lived near the railroad tracks. It watched the freight trains roar past its dog house every day. One day the dog decided to chase one of the freight trains and catch it. It waited until the train slowed for a sharp curve and then boldly positioned itself in the middle of the tracks. The big freight train came to a screeching halt only inches in front of the dog.

Once the dog had succeeded in stopping the train, it didn't know what to do with it. The engineer and brakeman yelled at the dog as they shooed it from the tracks and resumed their journey. In the end, "catching" the train didn't bring the dog the satisfaction it had thought it would. The dog probably would have been more fulfilled if it had chased and caught a rabbit.

Today, make sure that what you are pursuing is truly what you want, should you attain it. Though you may face difficulty or adverse circumstances in attaining your goal, don't despair. Ask for guidance, solicit advice, and persevere only if you can do so without compromising your values or identity. Only then will your direction be sure and your achievement fulfilling.

GOD'S Little Lessons for Teens

HAPPINESS

For to the man who pleases him God gives wisdom and knowledge and joy.

Ecclesiastes 2:26 RSV

A cheerful heart brings a smile to your face; a sad heart makes it hard to get through the day.

Proverbs 15:13 THE MESSAGE

"I have told you this so that my joy may be in you and that your joy may be complete."

John 15:11

Happy is the man that findeth wisdom, and the man that getteth understanding.

Proverbs 3:13 KJV

FROM SUICIDE TO SUNSHINE

There once was a man named Jeb. Early in his life, he was so miserable that he attempted to kill himself by drinking poison. His suicide attempt failed, however, and he succeeded only in burning his lips. As Jeb slowly recovered, he berated himself for his failure to kill himself. Yet as time passed, a different thought came to him: *Perhaps God has spared me for a purpose.*

From that moment on, Jeb decided it was his purpose in life to make others happy. Everywhere he went for the next thirty years, he left a trail of smiles and sunshine. He was one of the happiest people you could ever hope to meet. He handed everyone he met a business card on which he had printed this message:

THE WAY TO HAPPINESS

- Keep your heart free from hate, your mind free from worry.
- Live simply; expect little; give much; fill your life with love; scatter sunshine.
- Forget self.
- Think of others, and do as you would be done by.
- Try it for a week—you will be surprised.

Jeb's life could have ended in tragedy. Instead, God gave him a mission to help others find happiness. Are you helping others find happiness as well?

GOD'S Little Lessons for Teens

HAPPINESS

How blessed is the one whom Thou dost choose, and bring near to Thee, To dwell in Thy courts.

Psalm 65:4 NASB

It is possible to give freely and become more wealthy, but those who are stingy will lose everything.

Proverbs 11:24 NLT

A generous man will himself be blessed, for he shares his food with the poor.

Proverbs 22:9

Warn the rich people of this world not to be proud or to trust in wealth that is easily lost. Tell them to have faith in God, who is rich and blesses us with everything we need to enjoy life. Instruct them to do as many good deeds as they can and to help everyone. Remind the rich to be generous and share what they have. This will lay a solid foundation for the future, so that they will know what true life is like.

1 Timothy 6:17-19 CEV

THE WORLD WON'T MAKE YOU HAPPY

When the great golfer Babe Didrikson Zaharias was dying of cancer, her husband, George Zaharias, came to her bedside. Although he desired to be strong for her sake, he found he was unable to control his emotions and began to cry. Babe said to him gently, "Now, honey, don't take on so. While I've been in the hospital, I have learned one thing. A moment of happiness is a lifetime, and I have had a lot of happiness."

Happiness does not come wrapped in brightly colored packages as a "gift" given to us by others. Happiness comes when we uncover the gifts that lie within us and begin to use them to please God and bless others.

Happiness flows from within. It is found in the moments of life we label as "quality" rather than "quantity." George Bernard Shaw once said, "This is the true joy in life: being used for a purpose recognized by yourself as a mighty one."

The only person who can truly make you happy is yourself. You simply have to decide to be happy.

97

IMPURE THOUGHTS

*Set your mind on things above, not on things
on the earth.*

Colossians 3:2 NKJV

*Jesus turned on Peter and said . . . "You
are a dangerous trap to me. You are thinking
merely from a human point of view, and not
from God's."*

Matthew 16:23 TLB

*We pull down every proud obstacle that is raised
against the knowledge of God; we take every
thought captive and make it obey Christ.*

2 Corinthians 10:5 TEV

The thoughts of the wicked are *an abomination
to the LORD: but* the *words of the pure* are
pleasant words.

Proverbs 15:26 KJV

A WAY OF ESCAPE

As a teen, Megan arrived home from school just in time to watch an hour of soap operas before doing her homework. She enjoyed the escape into the TV world and wasn't really aware that the programs were creating in her an inordinate amount of sexual curiosity. Over months and even years of watching her "soaps," Megan's perspective on life shifted. She began to think, *Relationships don't need to be pure—in fact, the impure ones seem more exciting. Fidelity doesn't matter, as long as a person is "happy."*

As a college student, Megan found it easy to participate in "one-night stands." Then, after a short marriage ended in catastrophe as a result of her infidelity, she sought help from a counselor. At the outset, it was difficult for the counselor to understand why Megan had engaged in extramarital affairs. As far as her public behavior was concerned, she had been a model teenager at home, at church, and at school. Finally, the counselor discovered the source of the impurity that drove Megan to participate in her hidden life.

We can avert impurity and temptation by avoiding those things that cause it. But we are human, and no matter how careful we are, we will be tempted. Therefore, God always provides a way of escape!

IMPURE THOUGHTS

No temptation has overtaken you that is not common to man. God is faithful, and he will not let you be tempted beyond your strength, but with the temptation will also provide the way of escape, that you may be able to endure it.

1 Corinthians 10:13 RSV

Since he himself has gone through suffering and temptation, he is able to help us when we are being tempted.

Hebrews 2:18 NLT

You are of God, little children, and have overcome them, because He who is in you is greater than he who is in the world.

1 John 4:4 NKJV

You obeyed my message and endured. So I will protect you from the time of testing that everyone in all the world must go through.

Revelation 3:10 CEV

A MOTHBALLED CONSCIENCE

Norman Vincent Peale once stayed home for a month while his wife and children went on vacation. About midway through that month, Peale met a beautiful girl looking for excitement. When she made it clear that she would like to go on a date with Peale, he "put his conscience in mothballs" and arranged to meet her on Saturday night.

Peale awoke on Saturday morning and decided to take a walk on the beach. He took an old axe along to chop some rope away from the wreck of an old barge that had washed up on the shore. Due to the freshness of the morning and the rhythm of the axe, Peale began to chop in earnest.

As he chopped, a strange thing began to happen. He said, "I felt as if I were outside myself, looking at myself through a kind of fog that was gradually clearing. Suddenly I knew that what I had been planning for that evening was so wrong, so out of keeping with the innermost me." Peale promptly cancelled the date.

Take a good look at the choices you make. Promptly reconsider any that contradict your conscience, and ask God for a clearer view on the right way to proceed.

JEALOUSY

When you follow your own wrong inclinations
your lives will produce these evil results:
. . . hatred and fighting, jealousy and anger,
constant effort to get the best for yourself.

Galatians 5:19–20 TLB

A relaxed attitude lengthens life; jealousy
rots it away.

Proverbs 14:30 NLT

Let us behave decently, as in the daytime, not in
orgies and drunkenness, not in sexual immorality
and debauchery, not in dissension and jealousy.

Romans 13:13

Anger is cruel and destroys like a flood,
but no one can put up with jealousy!

Proverbs 27:4 NCV

BE A BEE

Some people let jealousy rule their emotions. They seem to go through their days with their "stingers out," ready to attack others or to defend their positions at the slightest provocation. We should remember, however, the full nature of the "bees" we sometimes seem to emulate.

Bees readily feed each other. The worker bees feed the queen bee, who cannot feed herself. They feed the drones while they work in the hive. They feed their young. They will even feed bees from different colonies. In cold weather, they cluster together for warmth. They fan their wings to cool the hive in hot weather, thus working for one another's comfort.

When the bees must move to new quarters, scouts report back to the group, performing a dance like the one used to report a find of flowers. When enough scouts have confirmed the suitability of the new location, the bees appear to make a common decision, take wing, and migrate together in what we call a swarm. Their communal caring for each other leaves no room for jealousy.

Bees engage their stingers only as a last-resort measure of self-defense, but they never use them against their fellow bees. We would do well to learn from them!

103

JEALOUSY

Jealousy enrages a man, And he will not spare in the day of vengeance.

Proverbs 6:34 NASB

When the Jewish leaders saw the crowds, they were jealous, and cursed and argued against whatever Paul said.

Acts 13:45 TLB

Jacob's sons became jealous of Joseph and sold him to be a slave in Egypt.

Acts 7:9 NCV

When there is jealousy among you and you quarrel with one another, doesn't this prove that you belong to this world, living by its standards?

1 Corinthians 3:3 TEV

MINING FOR GOLD

Andrew Carnegie, considered to be one of the first to emphasize self-esteem and the potential for inner greatness, was famous for his ability to produce millionaires from among his employees.

Carnegie knew how to bring about change in people. He inspired them to develop their hidden treasure within and then watched with encouragement as their lives became transformed. He responded to their growth with enthusiasm instead of envy.

Many times we respond to others' successes with a negative complaint of "Why them? Why not me?" Envious of someone else's position, status, or abilities, we may even resort to bitter comments about them. Our energies would be better spent reviewing our own lives and looking for the gold hidden inside ourselves.

We should follow Andrew Carnegie's example of encouraging others in their successes. If we adopt an attitude of enthusiasm instead of jealousy, everyone will benefit. The next time you have an opportunity to cheer for a friend who has accomplished something special, turn up the volume.

JOY

*My brethren, count it all joy when you fall
into various trials, knowing that the testing
of your faith produces patience.*

James 1:2-3 NKJV

*They that sow in tears shall reap in joy. He
that goeth forth and weepeth, bearing precious
seed, shall doubtless come again with rejoicing,
bringing his sheaves* with him.

Psalms 126:5-6 KJV

*May the righteous be glad and rejoice before
God; may they be happy and joyful.*

Psalm 68:3

*The kingdom of God is not eating and
drinking, but righteousness and peace
and joy in the Holy Spirit.*

Romans 14:17 NASB

A JOYFUL OUTLOOK

Legend says that when an architect went to check on the construction of the cathedral of Notre Dame, he encountered three different stone masons with identical jobs. He approached the first worker and asked, "What are you doing?"

The man snapped back, "Are you blind? I'm sweating under this blazing sun, cutting these impossible boulders with primitive tools, and putting them together the way I've been told."

The architect quickly backed off, retreated to a second worker, and asked the same question, "What are you doing?"

This worker replied matter-of-factly, "I'm shaping these boulders into usable forms, which are then assembled according to plan. It's hard, repetitive work, but I earn five francs a week, and that supports my wife and children. It could be worse, could be better."

Feeling somewhat encouraged, the architect went on to a third worker, asking, "What are you doing?"

The worker lifted his eyes to the sky, smiled, and said, "Why, can't you see? I'm building a beautiful cathedral for God!"

The third workman realized that every job can be done cheerfully. The joy you give to your work or study today will directly impact the satisfaction you feel at the day's end!

GOD'S Little Lessons for Teens

JOY

He will yet fill your mouth with laughter and your lips with shouts of joy.

Job 8:21

The redeemed of the LORD shall return, and come with singing unto Zion; and everlasting joy shall be upon their head: they shall obtain gladness and joy; and sorrow and mourning shall flee away.

Isaiah 51:11 KJV

You will show me the path of life; in Your presence is fullness of joy; at Your right hand are pleasures forevermore.

Psalm 16:11 NKJV

Let all those that put their trust in Thee rejoice: let them ever shout for joy.

Psalm 5:11 KJV

CRIES OF HALLELUJAH

Handel's masterpiece, *The Messiah,* has inspired millions through the centuries. Few know, however, that George Frederick Handel composed the piece in about three weeks. The music literally came to him in a flurry of notes and motifs. He composed feverishly, as if driven by the unseen Composer. It is also little known that Handel composed the work while his eyesight was failing and while he was facing a threat of debtor's prison because of outstanding bills.

He credits the completion of the work to one thing: joy. He was quoted as saying that he felt as if his heart would burst with joy at what he was hearing in his mind and soul. It was joy that compelled him to write, forced him to create, and ultimately found expression in the "Hallelujah Chorus."

Handel lived to see his oratorio become a cherished tradition and a popular work. He was especially pleased to see it performed to raise money for benevolent causes—to help the less fortunate relieve the stress of life with joy.

Take time today to find joy in your everyday tasks, in spite of your circumstances. Remember that God is busy creating a unique masterpiece out of your own life, so choose to be filled with joy!

GOD'S Little Lessons for Teens

KNOWLEDGE

*Praise God forever and ever, because he has
wisdom and power. . . . He gives wisdom to
those who are wise and knowledge to those
who understand.*

Daniel 2:20–21 NCV

*Wisdom and knowledge will be the stability of
your times,* And *the strength of salvation.*

Isaiah 33:6 NKJV

*O the depth of the riches both of the wisdom
and knowledge of God! how unsearchable* are
his judgments, and his ways past finding out!

Romans 11:33 KJV

*Wisdom will enter your heart, And knowledge
will be pleasant to your soul.*

Proverbs 2:10 NASB

THE BEST IS YET TO BE

At Columbia University, John Erskine was considered one of their greatest teachers ever. He was a true "Renaissance man"—author of sixty books, accomplished concert pianist, head of the Julliard School of Music, and a popular and witty lecturer.

Students flocked to Erskine's courses, not because of his fame or his accomplishments, but because his excitement for learning was contagious. He was possessed of a conviction that the world did not belong to him, but to his students.

Over and over he would remind them, "The best books are yet to be written. The best paintings have not yet been painted. The best governments are yet to be formed. The best is yet to be done—by you!"

Indeed, hundreds of John Erskine's students have gone into the world as leaders in every aspect of music—as teachers, performers, and composers. Others have become writers, painters, and political leaders. Many attribute their achievements and dreams to this mentor's reminder that the best is yet to be.

By reminding ourselves of the importance of education, we do our part to assure our future greatness.

GOD'S Little Lessons for Teens

KNOWLEDGE

A man of understanding and knowledge maintains order.

Proverbs 28:2

*The fear of the L*ORD* is the beginning of wisdom, and knowledge of the Holy One is understanding.*

Proverbs 9:10

You have an anointing from the Holy One, and all of you know the truth.

1 John 2:20

Grow in the grace and knowledge of our Lord and Savior Jesus Christ.

2 Peter 3:18 NASB

KNOWING WHERE TO PECK

One day, an intricate piece of equipment on an assembly line broke down. The company's best machinists were called in to diagnose the problem, but they couldn't fix the machine. Finally, they suggested a specialist be brought in. The master mechanic arrived, looked the apparatus over thoroughly, and then asked for the smallest hammer they had on hand. He tapped on a precise area of the machine with the hammer and said, "Turn on the power. It ought to work now." His small tap with the hammer had apparently released a jammed mechanism. Sure enough, the machine worked.

Later, when the specialist sent a bill for $100, the manager was astounded! It seemed an exorbitant fee for one small tap! The manager asked the specialist to send an itemized statement. He complied, but he didn't reduce his fee. The statement read: $1 for pecking; $99 for knowing where to peck.

Learning is a necessary process in life. Doctors must study for years to learn how to care for the human body. Automobile mechanics must stay current with the innovative trends in computer diagnostics. Recertification and retraining are a must for many careers. Put as much learning as you can into every day of your life. You'll have much more to draw upon later!

GOD'S Little Lessons for Teens

LAZINESS

A lazy man sleeps soundly—and he goes hungry!

Proverbs 19:15 TLB

We do not want you to become lazy, but to imitate those who through faith and patience inherit what has been promised.

Hebrews 6:12

Hard work will give you power; being lazy will make you a slave.

Proverbs 12:24 TEV

Warn those who are idle, encourage the timid, help the weak, be patient with everyone.

1 Thessalonians 5:14

HARD-WORKING FINGERPRINTS

When Joni Eareckson Tada was nominated to serve on the National Council on Disability, she was required to be fingerprinted by the FBI. Though she cooperated as best she could, the agent had a difficult time getting the prints off the pads of her fingers. Finally, after four or five tries, the agent looked at her, shook his head, and said, "Lady, I'm sorry, but you just don't have any tread on these fingers of yours."

The agent then turned Joni's hand over, so she could get a close look at her own fingers. She discovered that the pads of her fingers were smooth—no ridges showed at all. Joni asked the agent if he had run into this problem before. The agent replied that though he had not personally encountered this situation, he knew that the only folks without fingerprints are those who never use their hands. He explained that the ridges on fingers deepen with use. The hands of bricklayers, carpenters, typists, and homemakers who do a lot of dishes always have good prints.

You might think that hard work would wear off good fingerprints. Not so. Hard work enhances them; laziness wears them away. How deep are your fingerprints?

GOD'S Little Lessons for Teens

LAZINESS

The lazy catch no food to cook, but a hard worker will have great wealth.

Proverbs 12:27 NCV

The lazy man longs for many things but his hands refuse to work. He is greedy to get, while the godly love to give!

Proverbs 21:25-26 TLB

You sleep a little; you take a nap. You fold your hands and lie down to rest. Soon you will be as poor as if you had been robbed.

Proverbs 24:33-34 NCV

Respect those who work hard among you.

1 Thessalonians 5:12

EARN YOUR PAY

Charles Oakley, an NBA all-star, has a reputation for being one of basketball's best rebounders. It's his hard work, however, that has probably contributed the most to his outstanding sports career.

While other professional players seem to have frequent injuries or are sidelined for other reasons, Oakley hasn't missed a game in three years, even though he has absorbed a great deal of physical punishment and is often pushed or fouled. He puts in miles and miles each game, running up and down the court. He frequently dives into the stands for loose balls. According to Oakley, his tenacity has an origin—his grandfather Julius Moss.

Moss was a farmer in Alabama who did most of his fieldwork by hand, which left him with a body full of aches and pains. He could have complained, but instead, he merely laughed them off and went about his business. Oakley learned a lesson from that—nothing should prevent him from earning a day's pay.

Being focused, dedicated, and disciplined will make the difference between a mediocre life and a great life. Pay your way, and earn your pay.

LONELINESS

In peace I will both lie down and sleep, For Thou alone, O LORD, dost make me to dwell in safety.

Psalm 4:8 NASB

You find families for those who are lonely. You set prisoners free and let them prosper, but all who rebel will live in a scorching desert.

Psalm 68:6 CEV

I lie down and sleep; I wake again, because the LORD sustains me.

Psalm 3:5

Thou dost show me the path of life; in thy presence there is fulness of joy, in thy right hand are pleasures for evermore.

Psalm 16:11 RSV

MY DADDY IS HERE

David Elkind, the famous child psychologist and author of the best-selling *The Hurried Child,* tells this true story about his role as a parent:

I remember visiting my middle son's nursery school class, at the request of his teacher so that I could observe a "problem child" in the class. It so happened that I was sitting and observing a group of boys, including my son, who sat in a circle nearby. Their conversation went like this:

Child A: "My daddy is a doctor, and he makes a lot of money, and we have a swimming pool."

Child B: "My daddy is a lawyer, and he flies to Washington and talks to the president."

Child C: "My daddy owns a company, and we have our own airplane."

Then my son (with aplomb, of course): "My daddy is here."

The most important thing about loving someone is being there for them. And "being there" often literally means being there. No matter what, God will always "be there" for you.

GOD'S Little Lessons for Teens

LONELINESS

Turn to me and be gracious to me, For I am lonely and afflicted.

Psalm 25:16 NASB

Even if my father and mother abandon me, the Lord will hold me close.

Psalm 27:10 NLT

"Though the mountains be shaken and the hills be removed, yet my unfailing love for you will not be shaken nor my covenant of peace be removed," says the LORD, who has compassion on you.

Isaiah 54:10

The eternal God is thy refuge, and underneath are the everlasting arms.

Deuteronomy 33:27 KJV

LEARNING FROM ISOLATION

On July 22, 1996, a Japanese teenager set out in a thirty-foot yacht on a solo voyage across the Pacific Ocean. On September 13, fourteen-year-old Subaru Takahashi sailed under the Golden Gate Bridge—the youngest person in recorded history to make the 4,600-mile journey alone. Midway into his journey, the motor on his yacht quit. His battery died five days later. Amazingly, he made the last 2,790 miles of his trip under "sail" power alone.

To prepare for this trip, Takahashi spent five hundred hours of intensive training with yachting experts. Yet this was not his first solo voyage. He began canoeing at age five and crossed the nineteen-mile Sado Strait in the Sea of Japan in a solo canoe when he was only nine years old.

One of the challenges of a solo sailor's long voyage is the feeling of isolation. Rather than bemoan the loneliness of his venture, Takahashi made solitude his ally, marking the days with a deeper awareness of his abilities and a greater respect for creation. Solitude ultimately warmed his soul and strengthened his resolve.

Learn to use your time alone as a time for growth. This positive approach will keep you focused and help you achieve your goals.

GOD'S Little Lessons for Teens

LOVE

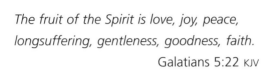

*The fruit of the Spirit is love, joy, peace,
longsuffering, gentleness, goodness, faith.*
Galatians 5:22 KJV

*Above all, love each other deeply, because l
ove covers over a multitude of sins.*
1 Peter 4:8

*Whoever loves is a child of God and knows
God. Whoever does not love does not know
God, for God is love.*
1 John 4:7–8 TEV

*I have loved you with an everlasting love;
Therefore I have drawn you with lovingkindness.*
Jeremiah 31:3 NASB

ETERNAL HARMONY

Centuries ago, a certain tribal leader was known for his great wisdom. In order to help his people live safely and peacefully, he carefully put laws into place guiding every aspect of tribal life.

In spite of those laws, there were problems. One day it came to the leader's attention that someone in the tribe was stealing.

"You know that the laws are for your protection, to help you live safely and in peace," he reminded them. "This stealing must stop. Therefore, the penalty has been increased from ten to twenty lashes from the whip for the person caught stealing."

When the thief continued to steal, the leader increased the penalty until finally it was forty lashes. Then a man came to say that the thief had been caught.

When the thief was bought to him the leader's face fell in shock and grief. It was his very own mother, old and frail. The leader spoke, "It is for our safety and peace. There must be forty lashes." The guards led his mother forward, and one began to unwind his whip. At the same moment, the leader stepped forward and wrapped his arms around his mother, shielding her with his own body.

A single moment, yet in it love and justice found an eternal harmony.

LOVE

We need have no fear of someone who loves us perfectly; his perfect love for us eliminates all dread.

1 John 4:18 TLB

"Love your enemies, do good, and lend, hoping for nothing in return; and your reward will be great."

Luke 6:35 NKJV

"This is my commandment, That ye love one another, as I have loved you."

John 15:12 KJV

Those who do not love their brothers and sisters, whom they have seen, cannot love God, whom they have never seen.

1 John 4:20 NCV

LOVE LOOKS DEEPER

During high school, Lynn became ill and missed two weeks of school. She returned to school to discover she had nine tests to make up in one week! When she got to the last test, she drew a total blank. She admitted to her teacher, "I don't know any of these answers."

Looking at her paper, the teacher said, "You know the answer to that! You answered a question I asked about that yesterday."

In spite of several hints, Lynn just could not remember. She finally said, "You're just going to have to fail me. I can't remember."

The teacher reached down with his red pencil, and as Lynn watched, he wrote a big, bold "A" at the top of the page.

"What are you doing?" Lynn asked.

Her teacher replied, "If you had been here and had time to study, that's what you would have earned. So that's what you are going to get."

Love takes into consideration the whole of who a person is, not just his or her mistakes or blunders. Love gives others a break once in a while. And that's an amazing gift to give to anyone.

MONEY/MATERIALISM

*The love of money is a root of all kinds of evil,
for which some have strayed from the faith in
their greediness, and pierced themselves
through with many sorrows.*

1 Timothy 6:10 NKJV

*Give me an eagerness for your decrees;
do not inflict me with love for money!*

Psalm 119:36 NLT

*Wisdom is a shelter as money is a shelter, but
the advantage of knowledge is this: that
wisdom preserves the life of its possessor.*

Ecclesiastes 7:12

*Instruct those who are rich in this present world
not to be conceited or to fix their hope on the
uncertainty of riches, but on God, who richly
supplies us with all things to enjoy.*

1 Timothy 6:17 NASB

MONEY, MONEY, MONEY

In 1923, eight of the most powerful money magnates in the world gathered for a meeting at the Edgewater Beach Hotel in Chicago, Illinois. The combined resources and assets of these eight men tallied more than the United States Treasury that year. In the group were the following men: Charles Schwab, president of a steel company; Richard Whitney, president of the New York Stock Exchange; Arthur Cutton, a wheat speculator; Albert Fall, a presidential cabinet member and a personally wealthy man; Jesse Livermore, the greatest Wall Street "bear" in his generation; Leon Fraser, president of the International Bank of Settlements; and Ivan Krueger, head of the largest monopoly in the nation. What an impressive gathering of financial eagles!

What happened to these men in later years? Schwab died penniless. Whitney served a life sentence in Sing Sing prison. Cutton became insolvent. Fall was pardoned from a federal prison so he might die at home. Fraser, Livermore, and Krueger committed suicide. Seven of these eight extremely rich men ended their lives with nothing.

Money is certainly not the answer to life's ills! Only God can give us peace, happiness, and joy. When we focus on God and His goodness, we can live content, knowing that He will meet all our needs.

MONEY/MATERIALISM

*"Don't store up treasures here on earth
where they can erode away or may be stolen.
Store them in heaven where they will never
lose their value."*

Matthew 6:19–20 TLB

*Stay away from the love of money; be satisfied
with what you have.*

Hebrews 13:5 NLT

*"Be careful and guard against all kinds of greed.
Life is not measured by how much one owns."*

Luke 12:15 NCV

*"No one can serve two masters. Either he will
hate the one and love the other, or he will
be devoted to the one and despise the other.
You cannot serve both God and Money."*

Matthew 6:24

POSSESSION OBSESSION

Many Americans have a possession obsession. Laptop computers, digital TVs, cell phones, sports cars—all the "right" stuff. These items aren't inherently bad, but they can easily become a source of false security, even pride.

The same danger exists with money. It's easy to become obsessed with all the things that money can buy. That's why it's important to remember that life is a journey. We never know what's around each curve, through each forest, across each river. Jesus taught His followers to travel light, taking with them only what they would need for their journey. He reminded them to concentrate on God's divine love. It provides a richness unmatched by any worldly possession. This love is so brilliant that it makes everything else pale in comparison. Materialism, on the other hand, is excess baggage that in the end only serves to make the journey burdensome.

There is nothing wrong with setting a goal to make money, but be careful not to let money make you into someone you don't like or cause you to do things you can't be proud of. Money should never be the most important thing in your life. When it is, it spoils everything else.

PATIENCE

*Be patient and wait for the L*ORD *to act; don't be worried about those who prosper or those who succeed in their evil plans.*

Psalm 37:7 TEV

It is better to be patient than to be proud. Don't become angry quickly, because getting angry is foolish.

Ecclesiastes 7:8–9 NCV

When the Holy Spirit controls our lives he will produce this kind of fruit in us: love, joy, peace, patience, kindness, goodness, faithfulness.

Galatians 5:22 TLB

Be completely humble and gentle; be patient, bearing with one another in love.

Ephesians 4:2

TEEN TYCOON

Twelve-year-old Michael sat on a beach and painstakingly put together a trotline—a maze of ropes to which several fish hooks can be attached. Meanwhile, his parents and two brothers were busy fishing. "You're wasting your time," they called. "Grab a pole and join in the fun."

Undaunted, Michael kept working at his tedious task, even though his family considered it of no value. At dinnertime, when everyone else was ready to call it a day, Michael cast his trotline far into the water, anchoring it to a stick he had plunged deep into the sand. During dinner, his family teased him about coming away from the day's fishing empty-handed. But after dinner, when Michael reeled in his trotline, there were more fish on his line than all of his family had caught put together.

In high school, Michael proved his patient persistence again when he bought his first computer and took it apart to figure out how it worked. Seventeen years later, Michael's patience had taken him from teen to tycoon. Michael Dell became the fourth-largest manufacturer of personal computers in America and the youngest man ever to head a Fortune 500 corporation.

Don't be afraid to start small. Work patiently and persistently. It's where you're headed that counts.

PATIENCE

*I waited patiently for the L*ORD *to help me,
and he turned to me and heard my cry.*

Psalm 40:1 NLT

---

*Let us lay aside every weight, and the sin which
doth so easily beset us, and let us run with
patience the race that is set before us.*

Hebrews 12:1 KJV

---

*Warn those who are unruly, comfort the
fainthearted, uphold the weak, be patient
with all.*

1 Thessalonians 5:14 NKJV

---

*The Lord is not slow about His promise, as
some count slowness, but is patient toward
you, not wishing for any to perish but for all
to come to repentance.*

2 Peter 3:9 NASB

PAINSTAKING PATIENCE

We often think of great artists and musicians as having "bursts" of genius. More often, they are models of painstaking patience. Their greatest works tend to have been accomplished over long periods and often because of extreme hardships. Consider the following:

- Beethoven is said to have rewritten each bar of his compositions at least a dozen times.
- Josef Haydn produced more than eight hundred musical compositions before writing *The Creation,* the oratorio for which he is most famous.
- Michelangelo's *Last Judgment* is considered one of the twelve master paintings of the ages. It took him eight years to complete and was the result of more than two thousand sketches and renderings.
- Leonardo de Vinci worked on *The Last Supper* for ten years, often working so diligently that he forgot to eat.
- When he was quite elderly, the pianist Ignace Paderewski still practiced six hours every day. When an admirer remarked that he must have a great deal of patience, Paderewski replied, "I have no more patience than the next fellow. I just use mine."

Are you a model of painstaking patience? Such persistence will pay you great dividends.

GOD'S Little Lessons for Teens

PEACE

The LORD gives his people strength. The LORD blesses them with peace.

Psalm 29:11 NLT

He will keep in perfect peace all those who trust in him, whose thoughts turn often to the Lord!

Isaiah 26:3 TLB

The peace that Christ gives is to guide you in the decisions you make; for it is to this peace that God has called you together in the one body.

Colossians 3:15 TEV

"I leave you peace; my peace I give you. I do not give it to you as the world does. So don't let your hearts be troubled or afraid."

John 14:27 NCV

THE MIRACULOUS BOMBSHELLS

During a run over Kasel, Germany, Elmer Bendiner's B-17 bomber took a barrage of flack from Nazi anti-aircraft. When he and his crew returned to base after a successful mission, he was amazed to learn that eleven 20-millimeter shells had pierced the fuel tank but did not cause even one explosion. Eleven unexploded shells? It seemed like a miracle.

The shells were sent to the armorers to be defused, after which intelligence officers came by to retrieve them. The armorers reported something even more mystifying. When they opened the shells, they found no explosive charge in any of them. They appeared to be empty and harmless.

One of the shells, however, was not completely empty. It contained a carefully rolled piece of paper. On it was scrawled a message in the Czech language of a prison camp worker: *This is all we can do for you now.* It was a miracle, all right, not of misfired shells, but of peace-loving hearts.

When you make a commitment to sow peace into the lives of others, you will reap back tremendous hope for your own life.

PEACE

Great peace have they who love your law,
and nothing can make them stumble.

Psalm 119:165

LORD, Thou wilt establish peace for us, Since
Thou hast also performed for us all our works.

Isaiah 26:12 NASB

Be perfect, be of good comfort, be of one
mind, live in peace; and the God of love and
peace shall be with you.

2 Corinthians 13:11 KJV

When a man's ways are pleasing to the LORD,
he makes even his enemies to be at peace
with him.

Proverbs 16:7 NASB

TUNED FOR PEACE

A Native American visited New York City. As he walked the busy streets with a friend, he suddenly stopped and said, "I hear a cricket."

The friend replied, "It's the noon hour. People are jammed on the sidewalks; cars are honking; the city is full of noise. And you think you can hear a cricket?"

"I'm sure I do," said the man. He listened more closely and then walked to the corner of a nearby building. There was a shrub growing in a large cement planter alongside the building. He dug into the leaves underneath the shrub and pulled out a cricket. His friend was astounded.

The Native American said, "The fact is that my ears are different than yours. It all depends on what your ears have been tuned to hear. Let me show you." At that, he reached into his pocket, pulled out a handful of loose change, and dropped the coins on the pavement. Every head within a half block turned toward the noise. "See what I mean?" he said, picking up the coins. "It all depends on what you are listening for."

Listen today to those things that will bring you peace. Heed those things that will prepare you for eternity.

GOD'S Little Lessons for Teens

PEER PRESSURE

We will not be influenced by every new teaching we hear from people who are trying to fool us. They make plans and try any kind of trick to fool people into following the wrong path.

Ephesians 4:14 NCV

I am afraid that someone may fool you with smooth talk. . . . Don't let others spoil your faith and joy with their philosophies, their wrong and shallow answers built on men's thoughts and ideas.

Colossians 2:4,8 TLB

Do not conform any longer to the pattern of this world, but be transformed by the renewing of your mind.

Romans 12:2

[Jesus said]: "I have set an example for you, so that you will do just what I have done for you."

John 13:15 TEV

EQUAL AND OPPOSITE

The bathysphere is an amazing invention. Operating like miniature submarines, bathyspheres have been used to explore the ocean in places so deep the water pressure would crush a conventional submarine as easily as if it were an aluminum can. Bathyspheres compensate for the intense water pressure with plates of steel several inches thick. The steel withstands the water pressure, but it also makes the bathysphere very heavy and hard to maneuver. The inside is tiny and cramped, allowing for only one or two people to survey the ocean floor through a tiny plate-glass window.

Amazingly, divers find fish and other sea creatures at every depth of the ocean! Some of these creatures are quite small and have normal-looking skin. No heavy metal for them! They swim freely, remaining flexible and supple in the inky waters.

How is it that fish can live at these depths without being crushed? They compensate for the outside pressure with equal and opposite pressure from inside.

Spiritual fortitude works in the same way. The greater the peer pressure we experience, the greater the need for us to allow God's power to work within us to exert an equal and opposite pressure.

PEER PRESSURE

*Your brother or your son or your daughter or the
wife you love or your closest friend may secretly
encourage you to worship other gods. . . . But
do not let any of them persuade you; do not
even listen to them.*

Deuteronomy 13:6,8 TEV

*Fully aware of God's death penalty for these
crimes . . . they went right ahead and did them
anyway, and encouraged others to do them, too.*

Romans 1:32 TLB

*Each of you should look not only to your own
interests, but also to the interests of others.
Your attitude should be the same as that of
Christ Jesus.*

Philippians 2:4–5

*In every way be an example of doing
good deeds.*

Titus 2:7 NCV

RESISTING THE RUTS

A biologist once placed several caterpillars on the rim of a pot that held a delicious (to a caterpillar) green plant. He lined them up head-to-tail with no break in the circular parade.

The tiny creatures walked around the rim of the pot for days until they died of exhaustion and starvation. Food was only inches away, but the follow-the-leader instinct was even stronger than the drive to eat and survive.

We sometimes find ourselves in similar situations, and when we do, we should ask ourselves three questions:

1. *Whom am I following?* We adopt certain patterns in our lives sometimes because of peer pressure. It's important to choose a wise leader to follow.

2. *Is this rut of my own making?* It's common to choose a rut because it's comfortable and avoids risk. If all else fails, choose a new rut!

3. *Where does this rut lead?* Ruts develop when we lose a sense of vision for our lives. Developing new goals will take us out of our ruts.

To resist the peer pressure in your life, obey the still, small voice within!

GOD'S Little Lessons for Teens

PRAYER

"When you pray, go away by yourself, all alone, and shut the door behind you and pray to your Father secretly, and your Father, who knows your secrets, will reward you."

Matthew 6:6 TLB

Even before they finish praying to me, I will answer their prayers.

Isaiah 65:24 TEV

"Believe that you have received the things you ask for in prayer, and God will give them to you."

Mark 11:24 NCV

The earnest prayer of a righteous person has great power and wonderful results.

James 5:16 NLT

PRAY YOUR STRESS AWAY

Claire Townsend found the weekly production meetings at the major motion picture studio where she worked to be extremely stressful. All morning, various department heads would jockey for position. The studio had just been purchased, jobs were uncertain, and team spirit had vanished. To counteract the stress, Claire began to spend more time praying. She was soon to discover the power of God's love in her life. Even so, she dreaded this weekly battle.

Then one day during a particularly tense meeting, she began to pray silently for each person around the table. As she prayed, she began to feel the love of God rising up in her, calming and relaxing her. As co-workers looked her way, Claire smiled. Within minutes, the tone of the meeting changed from confrontational to cooperative. As the group relaxed, they became more creative, and Claire began to regard the meetings as an opportunity to practice God's love.

In the midst of a stressful situation, turn to God. When you shift your focus to His love for you and others, your stress will be replaced with peace.

GOD'S Little Lessons for Teens

PRAYER

The eyes of the Lord watch over those who do right, and his ears are open to their prayers.

1 Peter 3:12 NLT

"When you are praying, if you are angry with someone, forgive him so that your Father in heaven will also forgive your sins."

Mark 11:25 NCV

Call unto me, and I will answer thee, and shew thee great and mighty things, which thou knowest not.

Jeremiah 33:3 KJV

When good people pray, the LORD listens.

Proverbs 15:29 TEV

UNLOCK THE DOORS

Early in the twentieth century, Harry Houdini won fame as an escape artist. He claimed he could be put in any jail cell in the country and set himself free within minutes. In town after town, he did just that!

One time, however, something went wrong. Houdini entered a jail cell in his street clothes. The heavy metal doors clanged shut behind him, and he took from his belt a concealed piece of strong but flexible metal. He set to work on the lock to his cell, but something seemed different about this particular lock. For thirty minutes he worked without results. An hour passed. This was long after the time that Houdini normally freed himself. He began to sweat in exasperation. Still, he could not pick the lock.

Finally, feeling failure closing in around him, Houdini cried out in frustration, "God, help me!" He collapsed backward against the jail cell door. To his amazement, the door swung open! It had never been locked in the first place!

How many times are challenges impossible—or doors locked—only because we think they are? When we set our minds and energy on God and ask for His help, we often find the impossible tasks turn into incredible achievements.

GOD'S Little Lessons for Teens

PRIDE

*To fear the L*ORD *is to hate evil; I hate pride and arrogance, evil behavior and perverse speech.*

Proverbs 8:13

"Everyone who exalts himself will be humbled, and he who humbles himself will be exalted."

Luke 18:14 NKJV

A man's pride will bring him low, But a humble spirit will obtain honor.

Proverbs 29:23 NASB

Pride leads to arguments; be humble, take advice and become wise.

Proverbs 13:10 TLB

YIELD YOUR PRIDE

While driving down a country road, a man came to a narrow bridge. In front of the bridge was a sign that read, "Yield." Seeing no oncoming cars, the man continued across the bridge and on to his destination. On his way back along this same route, the man came to the same one-lane bridge from the opposite direction. To his surprise, he saw another "Yield" sign posted there.

Curious, he thought. *I'm sure there was a sign posted on the other side.* Sure enough, when he reached the other side of the bridge and looked back, he saw the sign. Yield signs had been placed at both ends of the bridge so that the drivers from both directions would give each other the right of way. It appeared to be a reasonable way to prevent a head-on collision.

If you find yourself in a combative situation with someone else, don't let your pride keep you from yielding. If this person has more authority than you, your lack of submission will put you in a bad position. If you are of equal authority, an exercise of your power will only build resentment in a person better kept as an ally. In either circumstance, the best way to avoid a collision is to yield.

PRIDE

The patient in spirit is better than the proud in spirit.

Ecclesiastes 7:8 NKJV

Pride will destroy a person; a proud attitude leads to ruin.

Proverbs 16:18 NCV

Do not think of yourself more highly than you should. Instead, be modest in your thinking.

Romans 12:3 TEV

When pride comes, then comes disgrace, but with humility comes wisdom.

Proverbs 11:2

A TRUTHFUL TALE

The story is told of an old minister who survived the great Johnstown flood. He loved to tell the story over and over, usually in great detail. Everywhere he went, all he talked about was this great historic event in his life. Eventually, the minister died and went to Heaven.

In Heaven, he attended a meeting of saints who had gathered to share their life experiences. The minister was very excited, and he ran to ask Peter if he might relate the incredible story of his survival from the Johnstown flood.

Peter hesitated for a moment and then said, "Yes, you may share, but just remember that Noah will be in the audience tonight."

When you tell the tales of your life, it is always wise to remember that there may be people hidden somewhere in your audience who will know if what you say is true and accurate or merely prideful boasting. Those people might have been eyewitnesses to the event, or they may have had a similar experience, but on a much greater scale.

The best course is always to tell your experience as accurately as possible. Both understatements and exaggerations are prideful lies. Avoid them.

149

PRIORITIES

Trust in the LORD with all your heart; do not depend on your own understanding. Seek his will in all you do, and he will direct your paths.

Proverbs 3:5-6 NLT

The LORD has told us what is good. What he requires of us is this: to do what is just, to show constant love, and to live in humble fellowship with our God.

Micah 6:8 TEV

Decide today whom you will obey. . . . As for me and my family, we will serve the Lord.

Joshua 24:15 TLB

"He will give you all you need from day to day if you live for him and make the Kingdom of God your primary concern."

Matthew 6:33 NLT

ONE TO SIX

Charles Schwab, one of the first presidents of Bethlehem Steel, once asked an efficiency expert to help him be more productive at work. The expert told Schwab he could increase his productivity by at least 50 percent with a simple system. He then handed him a piece of paper and instructed him to write down the six most important tasks he would have to do the next day and number them in the order of their importance.

Then the man said, "Put this paper in your pocket. First thing tomorrow morning, look at the first item, and start working on it until it is finished. Then tackle the next item in the same way, and so on. Do this until quitting time every working day. After you've tried this system for a while, have your men try it. Then send me a check for what you think it's worth."

A few weeks later Schwab sent the expert a check for $25,000, calling his advice the most profitable lesson he had ever learned. And in just five years, largely by following this simple system, Bethlehem Steel became the largest independent steel producer in the world.

What are the six most important tasks you have to do tomorrow? Write them down, and accomplish them!

PRIORITIES

This is what the LORD says: "Stand at the crossroads and look; ask for the ancient paths, ask where the good way is, and walk in it, and you will find rest for your souls."

Jeremiah 6:16

Saul prayed to the LORD, the God of Israel, "Give me the right answer."

1 Samuel 14:41

"The more lowly your service to others, the greater you are. To be the greatest, be a servant."

Matthew 23:11 TLB

Respect the LORD your God, and do what he has told you to do. Love him. Serve the LORD your God with your whole being, and obey the Lord's commands and laws.

Deuteronomy 10:12-13 NCV

TO PLEASE THE MASTER

A young man once studied violin under a world-renowned violinist. He worked hard for several years perfecting his talent, and the day finally came when he was called upon to give his first major public recital in the large city where both he and his teacher lived. Following each selection, which he performed with great skill and passion, the performer seemed uneasy about the great applause he received. Even though he knew those in the audience were musically astute and not likely to give such applause to a less than superior performance, the young man acted almost deaf to the appreciation that was being showered on him.

At the close of the last number, the applause was thunderous, and numerous "Bravos" were shouted. The talented young violinist, however, had his eyes glued on only one spot. Finally, when an elderly man in the first row of the balcony smiled and nodded to him in approval, the young man relaxed and beamed with both relief and joy. His teacher had praised his work! The applause of thousands meant nothing until he had first won the approval of the master. His top priority was to please his teacher.

Whom are you most trying to please today?

PROTECTION

*You have done so much for those who come
to you for protection.*

Psalm 31:19 NLT

*When you pass through the waters, I will be
with you; And through the rivers, they will not
overflow you. When you walk through the fire,
you will not be scorched, Nor will the flame
burn you.*

Isaiah 43:2 NASB

*The eyes of the LORD run to and fro throughout
the whole earth, to show Himself strong on
behalf of those whose heart is loyal to Him.*

2 Chronicles 16:9 NKJV

*The Lord is faithful, and he will strengthen and
protect you from the evil one.*

2 Thessalonians 3:3

A KICK START

At a baby giraffe's birth, the newborn is hurled from its mother's body, falls ten feet, and lands on its back. Within seconds, it rolls to an upright position and tucks its legs under its body. The mother giraffe lowers her head long enough to take a quick look at her calf, and then she does what seems to be a very unreasonable thing: she kicks her baby and sends it sprawling head over heels. If it doesn't get up immediately, she kicks it again and again until the calf finally stands up on its wobbly legs.

Yet the mother giraffe isn't finished. She wants her baby to remember how it got up. So, as the newborn stands wobbling beside her, the mother giraffe kicks it off its feet!

In the wild, baby giraffes must be able to get up quickly in order to stay with the herd and avoid becoming a meal for predators. The best way a mother giraffe has of protecting her calf's life is for her to teach it to get up quickly and get moving.

Don't complain if the people who love you push you into action. They may be doing you a favor and protecting you from failure!

PROTECTION

He orders his angels to protect you wherever you go.

Psalm 91:11 NLT

The LORD thy God in the midst of thee is mighty; he will save, he will rejoice over thee with joy.

Zephaniah 3:17 KJV

He protects those who are loyal to him, but evil people will be silenced in darkness. Power is not the key to success.

1 Samuel 2:9 NCV

Let all who take refuge in you be glad; let them ever sing for joy. Spread your protection over them, that those who love your name may rejoice in you.

Psalm 5:11

A REAL
TRAFFIC-STOPPER

While driving along the freeway, the adults in the front seat of a car were talking when suddenly, they heard the horrifying sound of a car door opening, the whistle of wind, and a sickening thud. They quickly turned and saw that the three-year-old child riding in the back seat had fallen out of the car and was tumbling along the freeway. The driver screeched to a stop and then raced back toward her little girl. To her surprise, she found that all the traffic had stopped just a few feet away from her child. Her daughter had not been hit.

A truck driver drove the girl to a nearby hospital. The doctors there rushed her into the emergency room and soon came back with the good news: other than a few scrapes and bruises, the girl was fine—no broken bones, no apparent internal damage.

As the mother rushed to her child, the little girl opened her eyes and said, "Mommy, you know I wasn't afraid. While I was lying on the road waiting for you to get back to me, I looked up, and right there I saw Jesus holding back the traffic with His arms out."

God truly watches over us with loving care.

GOD'S Little Lessons for Teens

READING THE BIBLE

So shall My word be that goes forth from My mouth; It shall not return to Me void, But it shall accomplish what I please, And it shall prosper in the thing *for which I sent it.*

Isaiah 55:11 NKJV

Study to shew thyself approved unto God, a workman that needeth not to be ashamed, rightly dividing the word of truth.

2 Timothy 2:15 KJV

I have not neglected your instructions, because you yourself are my teacher.

Psalm 119:102 TEV

The teachings of the LORD are perfect; they give new strength. The rules of the LORD can be trusted; they make plain people wise.

Psalm 19:7 NCV

A LASTING LEGACY

Abraham Lincoln is often heralded as the greatest American president. His spirituality was undoubtedly the greatest reason for the decisions that led to his success, and he repeatedly referred to his indebtedness to and regard for the Bible.

Lincoln began reading the Bible in his boyhood. Its influence upon him increased over the years. Whenever he addressed the pubic, he quoted from the Bible more than from any other book. His literary style mirrored the style of the Bible, especially the writings of the prophets of Israel. His deeply moving second inaugural speech is strongly reminiscent of the book of Isaiah. He also thought in terms of biblical ideas and convictions, to an extent that has been unparalleled among modern statesmen.

Moreover, Lincoln was a man of prayer. Without apology or self-consciousness, he did not hesitate to request the prayers of others or acknowledge that he himself prayed often. He regarded prayer as a necessity and routinely spoke of seeking divine guidance, as though it was an entirely natural and reasonable thing to do.

Never curtail your pursuit of God. Never stop reading God's Word. It is the most important thing you can do to leave a lasting legacy of accomplishment and purpose.

READING THE BIBLE

*The whole Bible was given to us by inspiration
from God and is useful to teach us what is
true and to make us realize what is wrong
in our lives.*

2 Timothy 3:16 TLB

*Do not let this Book of the Law depart from
your mouth; meditate on it day and night, so
that you may be careful to do everything written
in it. Then you will be prosperous and successful.*

Joshua 1:8

*Your word is a lamp to my feet And a light
to my path.*

Psalm 119:105 NKJV

*The word of God is alive and active, sharper
than any double-edged sword. It cuts all the way
through, to where soul and spirit meet. . . . It
judges the desires and thoughts of the heart.*

Hebrews 4:12 TEV

ROOTED IN GOD

Psalm 1 describes two ways to view and experience life. One approach is scornful, negative, pessimistic, and cynical. The psalmist says those who live this way have shallow roots and will wither when a dry season comes because they have no true source of nourishment in their lives.

The other approach to life accepts the things of God and results in a life that is happy, principled, well grounded, and delightful. People who follow this way are likened to trees planted near steadily flowing streams. Their roots go deep and are always supplied with life-giving water even in times of trouble or drought.

The Bible clearly says that those who leave God out of their lives will not have staying power. Nothing will truly satisfy them. Nothing will seem worthwhile. Yet those who embrace God and the things of God will produce, multiply, and create things of lasting value for themselves and others.

What direction is your life going in today? How deep are your roots in God's soil? Are you planted beside His life-giving stream? If you wish to find true satisfaction, let the Bible's words shape your lifestyle.

RECONCILIATION

"If thy brother trespass against thee, rebuke him; and if he repent, forgive him."

Luke 17:3 KJV

"Whenever you stand praying, forgive, if you have anything against any one; so that you Father also who is in heaven may forgive you your trespasses."

Mark 11:25 RSV

The discretion of a man makes him slow to anger, And his glory is to overlook a transgression.

Proverbs 19:11 NKJV

"Do not resist an evil person. If someone strikes you on the right cheek, turn to him the other also."

Matthew 5:39

SILENCE BEYOND WORDS

Marie Louise de La Ramee writes in *Ouida:*

There are many moments in friendship, as in love, when silence is beyond words. The faults of our friend may be clear to us, but it is well to seem to shut our eyes to them. Friendship is usually treated by the majority of mankind as a tough and everlasting thing which will survive all manner of bad treatment. But this is an exceedingly great and foolish error; it may die in an hour of a single unwise word.

If the words "I love you" are the most important three words, then the words "I'm sorry" are probably the *two* most important! If you are willing to admit fault, there is a greater likelihood that others will do the same. Pursue peace in all of your relationships, and remember, sometimes silence is the best option.

REJECTION

The Lord will not forsake his people, for they are his prize.

Psalm 94:14 TLB

He who rejects this instruction does not reject man but God, who gives you his Holy Spirit.

1 Thessalonians 4:8

[Jesus said]: "Those the Father has given me will come to me, and I will never reject them."

John 6:37 NLT

Those who know you, LORD, will trust you; you do not abandon anyone who comes to you.

Psalm 9:10 TEV

TURNING REJECTION INTO OPPORTUNITY

Ernie was just out of school, eager to start his newspaper career, but he kept encountering rejection because of the age-old dilemma—he couldn't get a job because he lacked experience, and he couldn't get experience without a job.

He saw a classified ad for a position, which said applicants would be interviewed at 10 A.M. the next day. He worked all night to make his resumé look as promising as possible and prepared a portfolio of his writing samples. Arriving early the next morning, he was stunned to see a long line. He took his place at the end and recognized several older, more experienced reporters in front of him.

Ernie had an idea. He wrote a note and took it to the editor's secretary, telling her it was extremely important to show it to her boss immediately. When the editor read the note, he hurried through the rest of the interviews. It read, "Dear Sir, I'm the young man who is tenth in line. Please don't make any decisions until you see me."

This kind of resourcefulness was just what the editor was looking for in a reporter. Ernie had turned rejection into opportunity.

When you are faced with rejection, take a moment to learn something positive from this potentially painful experience. Then, use your rejection as a springboard to launch yourself into the next opportunity.

REJECTION

God will not reject a man of integrity, Nor will He support the evildoers.

Job 8:20 NASB

The LORD will not forsake His people, for His great name's sake, because it has pleased the LORD to make you His people.

1 Samuel 12:22 NKJV

You have been my helper. Do not reject me or forsake me, O God my Savior. Though my father and mother forsake me, the LORD will receive me.

Psalms 27:9-10

The LORD your God goes with you; he will never leave you nor forsake you.

Deuteronomy 31:6

THE WORTHLESS GLASS BULB

Years ago in a federal courtroom in New York, a sarcastic district attorney presented to a jury a glass gadget that looked something like a small electric light bulb. With great scorn and ridicule, the attorney accused the defendant of claiming that this "worthless device" might be used to transmit the human voice across the Atlantic!

The attorney alleged that gullible investors had been persuaded by preposterous claims to buy stock in the company—an obvious act of fraud. He urged the jury to give the defendant and his two partners stiff prison terms. Ultimately, the two associates were convicted, but the defendant was given his freedom after he received a severe scolding from the judge.

The defendant was inventor Lee de Forest. The "worthless glass bulb" that was also on trial was the audion tube he had developed—perhaps the single greatest invention of the twentieth century. It was the foundation for what has become a multi-billion-dollar electronics industry.

No matter how harsh the criticism or how stinging the sarcasm aimed at your original ideas, take them to their logical end. Either convince yourself that you were indeed wrong, or create something new!

GOD'S Little Lessons for Teens

RELATIONSHIPS

How sweet are your words to my taste,
sweeter than honey to my mouth!

Psalm 119:103

He who unites himself with the Lord is one
with him in spirit.

1 Corinthians 6:17

I will be a Father to you, and you will be my
sons and daughters, says the Lord Almighty.

2 Corinthians 6:18

Come near to God and he will come near
to you.

James 4:8

IT'S ALL ABOUT RELATIONSHIP

Imagine for a moment that someone you love comes to you and asks to borrow a small sum of money. You, no doubt, would lend it gladly, in part because of the close relationship you share.

Now imagine that this same person continues to come to you, asking for loans, food, clothing, the use of your car, a place to stay, and the use of your tools and appliances. While you do love this person, you would probably begin to feel that something was wrong. It's not the asking, but the attitude.

What causes the dilemma in this type of situation? The person who is coming with requests no longer sees his or her friend as someone with thoughts and feelings, but as a source of goods and services. So often we come to God in prayer with our request list in hand— "God, please do this . . ." or "God, I want . . . ." We are wise to reconsider our relationship with God in prayer. Who is this One to whom we pray? How good has He been to us? Doesn't He deserve our praise and thanksgiving?

We are missing out on the incredible benefits of an intimate relationship with God when we always come to Him with an empty hand, instead of a heart full of praise and thanksgiving.

169

RELATIONSHIPS

Do not be bound together with unbelievers;
for what partnership have righteousness and
lawlessness, or what fellowship has light
with darkness?

2 Corinthians 6:14 NASB

As iron sharpens iron, So a man sharpens
the countenance of his friend.

Proverbs 27:17 NKJV

Love one another deeply, from the heart.

1 Peter 1:22

Give everyone what you owe him: If you owe
taxes, pay taxes; if revenue, then revenue; if
respect, then respect; if honor, then honor.
Let no debt remain outstanding, except the
continuing debt to love one another.

Romans 13:7–8

REACH OUT
AND BUILD

Helen Keller suffered a fever as a baby that left her deaf, dumb, and blind. She overcame the difficult physical challenge of living with these handicaps and learned to read and write Braille. Her life inspired millions, and she was invited to visit every president in the White House from her childhood on.

What many people don't know, however, is how hard Helen worked as an adult to foster good relationships between sighted people and the blind. After graduating from Radcliffe College, Helen worked to help others until her death at the age of eighty-eight. She wrote numerous articles. She gave lectures and helped raise more than two million dollars for the American Foundation for the Blind. On her eightieth birthday, the American Foundation for Overseas Blind honored her by establishing the Helen Keller International Award for those who give outstanding help to the blind.

Not only are we called to overcome our own faults and limitations, but we are also asked to help build strong relationships with others. We are to use our talents for God's purposes, putting all our minds, hearts, and energies to the work He sets before us—strengthening relationships and building new ones as He gives us opportunity.

SELF-CONTROL

*Those who belong to Christ Jesus have nailed
the passions and desires of their sinful nature
to his cross.*

Galatians 5:24 NLT

*How can a young person live a pure life?
By obeying your word.*

Psalm 119:9 NCV

*Set a watch, O LORD, before my mouth;
keep the door of my lips. Incline not my
heart to any evil thing.*

Psalms 141:3-4 KJV

*I urge you therefore, brethren, by the mercies
of God, to present your bodies a living and
holy sacrifice, acceptable to God, which is
your spiritual service of worship.*

Romans 12:1 NASB

SILENCE IS GOLDEN

Three brawny, rough-looking fellows on huge roaring motorcycles pulled over and parked in front of the highway cafe. They came in and sat at the counter alongside a meek little guy who was reading his paper.

While waiting to order their meals, one of the toughs reached over and took a drink out of the little guy's coffee, then sneered at him, daring him to do anything about it. The little guy kept reading his paper. The second picked up a fork and speared the man's pork chop and devoured it. The third took a handful of salad and downed it in one bite, and all the while the little guy minded his own business.

Finally, with no food to eat, he got up, paid his bill, and walked out, leaving the bullies very dissatisfied and astounded by his actions.

We would be wise to learn from this man's behavior and to develop such self-control! When people try to provoke you, do not give them the satisfaction of an angry reply. Often times, the best response is silence. Harsh retaliation will only intensify the situation, and it will likely get you in to some sort of trouble. If you do choose to say something, choose your words carefully, and remember, "A gentle answer turns away wrath, but a harsh word stirs up anger" (Proverbs 15:1).

173

GOD'S Little Lessons for Teens

SELF-CONTROL

*Follow the Lord's rules for doing his work,
just as an athlete either follows the rules or
is disqualified and wins no prize.*

2 Timothy 2:5 TLB

*Knowing God leads to self-control. Self-control
leads to patient endurance, and patient
endurance leads to godliness.*

2 Peter 1:6 NLT

*Clothe yourselves with the Lord Jesus Christ,
and do not think about how to gratify the
desires of the sinful nature.*

Romans 13:14

*Do not let any unwholesome talk come out
of your mouths, but only what is helpful for
building others up according to their needs,
that it may benefit those who listen.*

Ephesians 4:29

KEEP YOUR EYES ON YOUR PRIZE

Henry Ford worked long hours in a little brick building behind his home, building the prototype for what would become the first Ford automobile. Enthusiasm and excitement fueled him, and he had to make himself stop to eat and sleep.

Then, even before he had completed this first model, Ford started thinking of ways to improve it. The thrill of what he was working on began to wane—why spend all this time finishing a car that's already inferior?

Something inside him compelled him to press on, as if he sensed he must focus his total energy on the first car and finish what he started. His concentration was rewarded—as he finished his original dream, he learned many new lessons about design and construction, which he later applied to the second car.

As a result, Henry Ford discovered a most important secret about life and work. The more completely you are able to focus on your present task, the more creatively you can envision future ones. Learn to be fully present in the moment, and let the next moment take care of itself.

GOD'S Little Lessons for Teens

SELF-DISCIPLINE

Do not give in to bodily passions, which are always at war against the soul.

1 Peter 2:11 TEV

Everything in the world—the cravings of sinful man, the lust of his eyes and the boasting of what he has and does—comes not from the Father but from the world.

1 John 2:16

Let my heart be blameless regarding Your statutes, That I may not be ashamed.

Psalm 119:80 NKJV

Those who belong to Christ Jesus have crucified their own sinful selves. They have given up their old selfish feelings and the evil things they wanted to do.

Galatians 5:24 NCV

GIVE YOURSELF A CHECK-UP

A boy walked into a drugstore one day and asked to use the telephone. He dialed a number and said, "Hello, Dr. Anderson, do you want to hire a boy to cut your grass and run errands for you?" After a pause he said, "Oh, you already have a boy? Are you completely satisfied with the job he's doing?" Another pause. "All right then, good-bye, Doctor."

As the boy thanked the druggist and prepared to leave, the druggist called to him. "Just a minute, son. I couldn't help but overhear your conversation. If you are looking for work, I could use a boy like you."

"Thank you, sir," the boy replied, "but I already have a job."

"You do?" the druggist responded. "But didn't you just try to get a job from Dr. Anderson?"

"No, sir," the boy said. "I already work for Dr. Anderson. I was just checking up on myself."

A self-disciplined individual looks for ways to improve performance and avoid mistakes. Ask those with whom and for whom you work to give you suggestions on how you might do better, achieve more, and grow to the next level. When you check up on yourself, others won't feel it is necessary to do so!

SELF-DISCIPLINE

*But I discipline my body and bring it into
subjection, lest, when I have preached to
others, I myself should become disqualified.*

1 Corinthians 9:27 NKJV

*I have been crucified with Christ; and it is no
longer I who live, but Christ lives in me; and the
life which I now live in the flesh I live by faith in
the Son of God, who loved me, and delivered
Himself up for me.*

Galatians 2:20 NASB

*He that hath no rule over his own spirit is like
a city that is broken down, and without walls.*

Proverbs 25:28 KJV

*Clothe yourselves with the Lord Jesus Christ,
and do not think about how to gratify the
desires of the sinful nature.*

Romans 13:14

ALL WE DID

O nce upon a time there was a little boy who was given everything he wanted. As an infant, he was given a bottle at the first little whimper. He was picked up and held whenever he fussed. His parents said, "He'll think we don't love him if we let him cry."

He was never disciplined for leaving the yard, even after being told not to. He suffered no consequence for breaking windows or tearing up flowerbeds. His parents said, "He'll think we don't love him if we stifle his will."

His mother picked up after him and made his bed. His parents said, "He'll think we don't love him if we give him chores."

Nobody ever stopped him from using bad words. He was never reprimanded for scribbling on his bedroom wall. His parents said, "He'll think we don't love him if we stifle his creativity."

He never was required to go to church. His parents said, "He'll think we don't love him if we force religion down his throat."

One day the parents received news that their son was in jail on a felony charge. They cried to each other, "All we ever did was love him and do things for him." Unfortunately, that is, indeed, *all* they did.

SELF-PITY

Those who wait on the LORD Shall renew their strength; They shall mount up with wings like eagles, They shall run and not be weary, They shall walk and not faint.

Isaiah 40:31 NKJV

"Peace I leave with you, my peace I give unto you: not as the world giveth, give I unto you. Let not your heart be troubled, neither let it be afraid."

John 14:27 KJV

I will give them a crown to replace their ashes, and the oil of gladness to replace their sorrow, and clothes of praise to replace their spirit of sadness.

Isaiah 61:3 NCV

I have learned, in whatsoever state I am, therewith *to be content.*

Philippians 4:11 KJV

DIFFERENT OUTLOOK, DIFFERENT OUTCOME

Kevin was a high school football star and later, an avid wrestler, boxer, hunter, and skin-diver. Then tragically, a broken neck left him paralyzed from the chest down. His doctors were hopeful that one day, with therapy, he would be able to walk with the help of braces and crutches.

The former athlete could not reconcile himself to his physical limitations, however, so he prevailed upon two of his friends to leave him alone in a wooded area. After they left, he held a twelve-gauge shotgun to his abdomen and pulled the trigger, committing suicide at the age of twenty-four.

At the age of nineteen, Jim was stabbed, leaving him paralyzed from the middle of his chest down. Although confined to a wheelchair, he lives alone, cooks his own meals, washes his clothes, and cleans his house. He drives himself in a specially equipped automobile. He has written three books and was the photographer for the first book on the history of wheelchair sports. Thirty years after his injury, he made a successful parachute jump, landing precisely on his target.

Kevin and Jim had nearly identical injuries and physical limitations. Their outlook, however, led to vastly different outcomes. What is your outlook on life today?

SELF-PITY

We are afflicted in every way, but not crushed;
perplexed, but not despairing; persecuted, but
not forsaken; stuck down, but not destroyed.

2 Corinthians 4:8-9 NASB

"Let not your heart be troubled; you believe
in God, believe also in Me."

John 14:1 NKJV

God has made us what we are. In Christ Jesus,
God made us to do good works, which God
planned in advance for us to live our lives doing.

Ephesians 2:10 NCV

We say with confidence, "The Lord is my helper;
I will not be afraid. What can man do to me?"

Hebrews 13:6

DON'T DESPAIR

While in the midst of contending with the geographic problems of building the Panama Canal, Colonel George Washington Goethals had to endure a great deal of criticism from those back home who predicted he would never complete his great task. The visionary builder continued on, refusing to give in to their doomsday attitudes or to succumb to self-pity because of their carping.

"Aren't you going to answer your critics?" a reporter asked him.

"In time I will," Goethals replied.

"How? And when?" the reporter inquired.

The colonel merely smiled and said simply, "I'll answer my detractors with a finished canal."

In the same way Ole Bull, a violinist in the nineteenth century, was once offered space in the *New York Herald* to answer his critics. He said, "I think it is best that they write against me. I shall play against them."

The finest response to your detractors is to faithfully do the very best you can do—consistently, persistently, and insistently. Don't waste time in self-pity. Make your steady, faithful work your best defense.

SEXUAL PRESSURE

*Each of you should learn to control his own
body in a way that is holy and honorable,
not in passionate lust like the heathen, who
do not know God.*

1 Thessalonians 4:4–5

*Our bodies were not made for sexual immorality.
They were made for the Lord, and the Lord
cares about our bodies.*

1 Corinthians 6:13 NLT

*Since you are God's people, it is not right that
any matters of sexual immorality or indecency
or greed should even be mentioned among you.*

Ephesians 5:3 TEV

*God did not call us to be impure, but to live a
holy life.*

1 Thessalonians 4:7

PROMISCUITY PRODUCES PAIN

The 1960s were known for many rebellions, among them the sexual revolution. "Free love" spilled over from the hippie movement into the mainstream of American culture. Premarital sexual experiences sanctioned by the "new morality" were openly flaunted. Extramarital affairs were excused. Multiple sex partners became an accepted norm in hippie communes.

One of the unexpected results of this trend, however, received little publicity. Dr. Francis Braceland, past president of the American Psychiatric Association and editor of the American Journal of Psychiatry, reported that an increasing number of young people were admitted to mental hospitals during this time. In discussing this finding at a National Methodist Convocation on Medicine and Theology, Braceland concluded, "a more lenient attitude about premarital sex imposed stresses on some college women that were severe enough to cause emotional breakdown."

Looking back over the years since the "new morality" has been accepted by a high percentage of Americans, one finds a rising number of rapes, abortions, divorces, premarital pregnancies, and single-family homes. Cases of sexually transmitted diseases, including herpes and HIV, have more than tripled in some areas. Coincidence? Perhaps, but the evidence is compelling. God's laws were meant to spare us the pain of poor choices and deadly consequences.

SHAME

*There is therefore now no condemnation for
those who are in Christ Jesus.*

Romans 8:1 NASB

*Work hard so God can approve you. Be a good
worker, one who does not need to be ashamed
and who correctly explains the word of truth.*

2 Timothy 2:15 NLT

Fear not; you will no longer live in shame.

Isaiah 54:4 NLT

*May those who hope in you not be disgraced
because of me, O Lord, the LORD Almighty;
may those who seek you not be put to shame.*

Psalm 69:6

SHAME AND BETRAYAL

Meg and Ann had been best friends since elementary school. Then one day, Meg told Ann that John had asked her for a date. Ann was disappointed because she'd had a crush on him for two years. Still, she managed to say, "Have a good time," and later, she put on a happy face as they became a constant twosome.

As the months passed, the girls remained close. Ann enjoyed teasing and laughing with John, so when she found herself alone with him one day, she did not hesitate to betray Meg's trust. Afterward, she felt sick inside. Deep shame welled up within her.

A few minutes of flirtation and passion resulted in a great deal of misery for her. She might never have known happiness again if Meg hadn't confronted her about her anti-social behavior and refusal to date. Ann sobbed, "I'm horrible. You don't know how I've wronged you." Meg said, "I do know, Ann," and one look into her eyes confirmed that she had known, had loved, and had forgiven. With that forgiveness, months of shameful pain melted away.

Shame is painful and debilitating. It can literally ruin a life. And forgiveness is the only lasting cure.

SPIRITUAL GROWTH

Let us stop going over the same old ground again and again, always teaching those first lessons about Christ. Let us go on instead to other things and become mature in our understanding, as strong Christians ought to be.

Hebrews 6:1 TLB

Practice these things and devote yourself to them, in order that your progress may be seen by all.

1 Timothy 4:15 TEV

Study to shew thyself approved unto God, a workman that needeth not to be ashamed, rightly dividing the word of truth.

2 Timothy 2:15 KJV

Open my eyes to see the wonderful truths in your law.

Psalm 119:18 NLT

DEEP ROOTS

Many people see abundant spring rains as a great blessing to farmers, especially if the rains come after the plants have sprouted and are several inches tall. What they don't realize is that even a short drought can have a devastating effect on a crop of seedlings that has received too much rain.

Why? Because during frequent rains, the young plants are not required to push their roots deeper into the soil in search of water. If a drought occurs later, plants with shallow root systems will quickly die.

We often receive abundance in our lives—rich fellowship, great teaching, thorough "soakings" of spiritual blessings. Yet when stress or tragedy enters our lives, we may find ourselves thinking God has abandoned us or is unfaithful. The fact is, we have allowed the "easiness" of our lives to keep us from pushing our spiritual roots deeper. We have allowed others to spoon-feed us, rather than develop our own deep, personal relationship with God through prayer and study of His Word.

Only the deeply rooted are able to endure hard times without wilting. The best advice is to enjoy the "rain" while seeking to grow even closer to Him.

GOD'S Little Lessons for Teens

STABILITY

He will not fear evil tidings; His heart is steadfast, trusting in the LORD.

Psalm 112:7 NASB

Grass withers and flowers fade, but the word of our God endures forever.

Isaiah 40:8 TEV

He who doubts is like a wave of the sea, blown and tossed by the wind. . . . he is a double-minded man, unstable in all he does.

James 1:6,8

When there is moral rot within a nation, its government topples easily; but with honest, sensible leaders there is stability.

Proverbs 28:2 TLB

A PROMISE KEPT

Stephen Covey once counseled a man who had a reputation for procrastination and selfishness. The man could rarely be counted on to keep his commitments. Covey challenged him to a simple change. "Will you get up in the morning when you say you're planning to get up?" Covey asked. "Will you just get up in the morning?"

The man saw little point in what Covey was challenging him to do, but when Covey asked him to commit to getting up at a certain time for a week, the man agreed to do so.

Covey saw the man a week later and asked, "Did you do it?" The man replied in the affirmative, so Covey then asked, "What's the next thing you're going to commit to do?"

Little by little, the man began to make and keep commitments. No one knew of the plan but Covey and one friend. Over time, the man made remarkable changes. His relationships improved, his promises were kept, and his integrity was regained. His entire life stabilized because he began to keep his promises—first to himself and then to others. When you keep your word to yourself, it becomes easier to keep your word to others, and it produces tremendous peace of mind and stability in your life.

STEWARDSHIP

Now it is required that those who have been given a trust must prove faithful.

1 Corinthians 4:2

"He who is faithful in what is least is faithful also in much; and he who is unjust in what is least is unjust also in much."

Luke 16:10 NKJV

"When you give to the needy, do not let your left hand know what your right hand is doing, so that your giving may be in secret."

Matthew 6:3-4

God has given gifts to each of you from his great variety of spiritual gifts. Manage them well so that God's generosity can flow through you.

1 Peter 4:10 NLT

STEWARDSHIP STARTS IN THE HEART

O seola McCarty practiced stewardship her entire life by helping people look nice. You see, she took in bundles of dirty clothes and washed and ironed them. She started after having to drop out of school in the sixth grade, and she continued her work into her eighties.

Oseola never married, never had children. And for most of her eighty-seven years, she spent almost no money. She lived in her old family home and wore simple clothes. She saved her money, most of it dollar bills and change, until she had amassed more than $150,000. Even more amazing was the fact that Oseola gave her entire savings to black college students across the state of Mississippi.

"I know it won't be too many years before I pass on," she explained, "and I wanted to share my wealth with the children."

Before her death, Oseola was able to witness a number of "her children" graduate from college with the help of her financial support. She teaches us all that stewardship starts in the heart, and when our hearts are full of love and generosity, God will show us a way to leave a legacy.

GOD'S Little Lessons for Teens

STRENGTH

You have armed me with strength for the battle;
you have subdued my enemies under my feet.

2 Samuel 22:40 NLT

The LORD gives strength to those who are weary.

Isaiah 40:29 CEV

My flesh and my heart may fail, but God is the
strength of my heart and my portion forever.

Psalm 73:26

I can do everything through him who gives
me strength.

Philippians 4:13

HE'LL CATCH YOU

When Walter Wangerin was a boy, he told all of his friends that his father was the strongest man alive. Then came the day when Wally climbed to the top of the backyard cherry tree. A storm blew up suddenly, and Wally was trapped. "Daddy!" he shouted, and instantly, his father appeared.

"Jump, and I'll catch you," he said.

Wally was frozen with fear. His big, strong dad looked quite small and frail down there on the ground, two skinny arms reaching out to catch him. Wally thought, *If I jump, and Dad doesn't catch me, I'll hit the ground and die!* "No!" he screamed back. At that moment the limb Wally was clinging to cracked at the trunk. Wally surrendered. He didn't jump—he fell—straight into Dad's ready arms. Crying and trembling, Wally wrapped his arms and legs around his father. Dad was strong after all. Up to that point, it had only been a theory. Now, it was a reality; it was experience.

Prayer is about surrendering our strength to God's strength, giving up our desires to take on God's desires, and obeying when He asks us to jump into His waiting arms.

195

STRENGTH

In returning and rest shall ye be saved;
in quietness and in confidence shall be
your strength.

Isaiah 30:15 KJV

I pray that out of his glorious riches he may
strengthen you with power through his Spirit
in your inner being, so that Christ may dwell
in your hearts through faith.

Ephesians 3:16–17

They that wait upon the Lord shall renew their
strength. They shall mount up with wings like
eagles; they shall run and not be weary; they
shall walk and not faint.

Isaiah 40:31 TLB

The LORD is my light and my salvation; whom
shall I fear? the LORD is the strength of my life;
of whom shall I be afraid?

Psalm 27:1 KJV

STRONG ROOTS

Consider these facts about trees and roots:

- Forestry experts estimate that the root spread of many trees is equal to the spread of their branches.

- As much as one-tenth of a tree is concealed in its roots.

- The combined length of the roots of a large oak tree would total several hundred miles.

- Hair-like as some tree roots are, an entire system of them can still exert tremendous pressure, uprooting boulders that weigh many tons.

- A tree's root system serves two functions: to anchor the tree and to collect moisture, without which the tree could not thrive.

- A tree's roots adapt to strengthen it against whatever may try to attack it. If it is wind, the roots grow thick and deep. If it is drought, the roots grow toward water.

People have "roots," too, and our roots have a direct effect on our branches and our fruit. Our roots are established in the inward matters of life, our thoughts and motives, and they enable us to produce strength on the outside. Are you building strong roots?

STRESS

"Come to Me, all you who labor and are heavy laden, and I will give you rest."

Matthew 11:28 NKJV

The peace of God, which passeth all understanding, shall keep your hearts and minds through Christ Jesus.

Philippians 4:7 KJV

You will keep in perfect peace him whose mind is steadfast, because he trust in you. Trust in the LORD forever, for the LORD, the LORD, is the Rock eternal.

Isaiah 26:3-4

May the Lord of peace himself always give you his peace no matter what happens. The Lord be with you all.

2 Thessalonians 3:16 NLT

THE RIGHT RESULTS

S adie Delaney's father taught her to try to do better than her competition. Shortly before she received her teaching license, a supervisor came to watch her and two other student teachers. Their assignment was to teach a class to bake cookies. Since the supervisor didn't have time for each student teacher to go through the entire lesson, she assigned a portion of the lesson to each one of them. Sadie was assigned to teach the girls how to serve and clean up.

The first student teacher panicked and forgot to halve the recipe and preheat the oven. The second girl was so behind because of the first girl's errors that the students made a mess in forming and baking the cookies.

Then it was Sadie's turn. She said to the girls, "We'll have to work together as a team." They quickly baked the remaining dough. Several girls scrubbed pans as soon as the cookies came out of the oven. Within ten minutes, they had several dozen perfect cookies and a clean kitchen. The supervisor was so impressed she offered Sadie a substitute teacher's license on the spot.

Do what it takes to get right results. Your life will be marked with less stress and more success!

GOD'S Little Lessons for Teens

SUCCESS

You will decide on a matter, and it will be established for you, and light will shine on your ways.

Job 22:28 RSV

Wealth and Glory accompany me—also substantial Honor and a good Name.

Proverbs 8:18 THE MESSAGE

True humility and fear of the LORD lead to riches, honor, and long life.

Proverbs 22:4 NLT

Suppose you are very rich and able to enjoy everything you own. Then go ahead and enjoy working hard—this is God's gift to you.

Ecclesiastes 5:19 CEV

OPPORTUNITY IS WAVING AT YOU

A young man from Kansas City had a deep desire to become an illustrator. He approached every newspaper and magazine he knew of, trying to sell his cartoons. Each editor quickly and coldly turned him down, implying that he ought to try another line of work.

Then one day a minister hired him part-time to design advertisements for church events. It was hardly the opportunity of a lifetime, but he started working from a small shed behind the church, doing the drawings he was hired to produce and also idly sketching whatever objects caught his eye, including the mice that scampered around the shed.

One of the mice became the subject of a cartoon the artist named "Mickey." Eventually it became the most famous cartoon character in the world, and its creator, Walt Disney, became one of our century's most successful innovators.

Somewhere within your sight and reach right now may lie some ordinary object that could transform your life. The question is: Are you looking? Are you ready and willing to go after the opportunities that are waving at you until you find a successful path for your life?

SUCCESS

True humility and respect for the Lord lead a man to riches, honor and long life.

Proverbs 22:4 TLB

And, of course, it is very good if a man has received wealth from the Lord, and the good health to enjoy it. To enjoy your work and to accept your lot in life—that is indeed a gift from God.

Ecclesiastes 5:19 TLB

Riches and honor are with me, enduring wealth and prosperity. My fruit is better than gold, even fine gold, and my yield than choice silver.

Proverbs 8:18-19 RSV

Wealth and riches are in his house, and his righteousness endures forever.

Psalm 112:3

FULFILLING YOUR PURPOSE

At forty-three, Lenny felt the time had come to give something back to his community, so he volunteered at a feeding program for homeless people. Soon he was counseling the families who came for food, directing them to places that provided shelter, and helping several of the men find jobs. The director of the program told him he had a talent for working with people and encouraged him to develop it.

Lenny had been working in a semi-clerical position as an administrative aide to a corporate executive. There wasn't any higher place he could go in his field. His one regret had been that he had never gone to college. Armed with the encouraging words of his fellow volunteers, he and his wife sold their home and went back to school. They both eventually earned doctoral degrees and became full-time family therapists. They opened a clinic together and rebuilt their lives, this time enjoying a much greater sense of personal fulfillment.

It's never too late to start a new career. And it's never too late to make a new start in your spiritual life. Genuine success is found in establishing a relationship with God, discovering who He created you to be, then developing the talents and gifts He has given you!

203

TEMPTATION

*No temptation has overtaken you that is not
common to man. God is faithful, and he will not
let you be tempted beyond your strength, but
with the temptation will also provide the way of
escape, that you may be able to endure it.*

1 Corinthians 10:13 RSV

*Since he himself has gone through suffering and
temptation, he is able to help us when we are
being tempted.*

Hebrews 2:18 NLT

*"Lead us not into temptation, but deliver
us from evil: For thine is the kingdom, and the
power, and the glory, for ever. Amen."*

Matthew 6:13 KJV

*Consider him who endured such opposition
from sinful men, so that you will not grow
weary and lose heart. In your struggle against
sin, you have not yet resisted to the point of
shedding your blood.*

Hebrews 12:3-4

STAY OUT OF THE PIG PEN

Farmers have a saying that goes something like, "Once you're standing in the pig pen, it's a little too late to worry about soiling your Sunday clothes." And that sound piece of advice carries beyond the farm. The key to avoiding wrong doing and compromise is to decide in advance to stay as far away from it as possible.

Impropriety has a way of revealing itself a little at a time. Once we get to thinking that some form of wrong doing is "not so bad," it's often just a few more steps to the pig pen, with little hope of escaping without getting dirty.

Promise God and yourself right now that you will resist even the appearance of wrong doing whenever you encounter it. Decide ahead of time how you would handle hypothetical situations. Would you cheat on a test? Would you lie to your parents? Don't listen to people who say, "Everybody's doing it." Everybody isn't!

Everyone encounters temptation. It's a fact of life. But you can successfully overcome temptation by identifying the "pig pens" you must face each day and by determining to stay as far away from them as possible. Remember that an ounce of prevention can be worth ten pounds of purity.

TRAGEDY

Though you have made me see troubles, many
and bitter, you will restore my life again.

Psalm 71:20

This is my comfort in my affliction, For
Your word has given me life.

Psalm 119:50 NKJV

*I cried out to the L*ORD *in my great trouble,*
and he answered me. I called to you from the
*world of the dead, and L*ORD*, you heard me!*

Jonah 2:2 NLT

We know that in everything God works for
the good of those who love him.

Romans 8:28 NCV

THE GIFT OF LIFE

Once a nationally syndicated columnist and now an author, Anna Quindlen seems to have enjoyed success at everything she has attempted. However, in taking a fellow commentator to task after he made light of teenage problems, Anna was reminded of the two attempts she had made to end her own life at age sixteen. She writes, "I was really driven through my high school years. I always had to be perfect in every way, ranging from how I looked to how my grades were. It was too much pressure."

In the early 1970s, Anna's mother died from ovarian cancer. This tragedy cured Anna of any desire to commit suicide. Her attitude toward life changed. "I could never look at life as anything but a great gift. I realized I didn't have any business taking it for granted."

When we are faced with the realization that life is temporary, we can finally come to grips with what is important. When we face our own immortality, our priorities quickly come into focus.

Consider your life as God's gift to you. Every moment is precious, so cherish them all. In doing so, you'll find purpose and meaning for each day.

TRUTH

Now, O LORD GOD, Thou art God, and Thy words are truth.

2 Samuel 7:28 NASB

Do not testify falsely against your neighbor.

Exodus 20:16 NLT

The words of the LORD are flawless, like silver refined in a furnace of clay, purified seven times.

Psalm 12:6

The LORD hates . . . A proud look, A lying tongue, Hands that shed innocent blood.

Proverbs 6:16-17 NKJV

SUCH A GOOD FEELING

Author Alice Walker once accidentally broke a fruit jar. Though there were several siblings around who could have done it, Alice's father turned to her and asked, "Did you break the jar, Alice?"

Alice said, "Looking into his large brown eyes, I knew that he wanted me to tell the truth. I also knew he might punish me if I did. But the truth inside of me wanted badly to be expressed. So I confessed."

Her father realized that the broken jar was an accident, so no punishment was administered. Yet what impressed Alice was the love she saw in her father's eyes when he knew that Alice had told the truth. "The love in his eyes rewarded and embraced me," Alice recalled. "Suddenly I felt an inner peace that I still recall with gratitude to this day whenever I am called upon to tell the truth."

A person always feels good after telling the truth, doing the noble thing, showing kindness, or meeting a need. We must remember, however, that we are to do what is right because it is right, not because it will make us feel better or bring us a reward—and that, is the truth.

209

TRUTH

*We will lovingly follow the truth at all times—
speaking truly, dealing truly, living truly—and so
become more and more in every way like Christ.*
                              Ephesians 4:15-16 TLB

*Jesus answered, "I am the way and the truth
and the life. No one comes to the Father
except through me."*
                              John 14:6

*Surely you heard of him and were taught in him
in accordance with the truth that is in Jesus.*
                              Ephesians 4:21

*All Scripture is inspired by God and is useful for
teaching the truth, rebuking error, correcting
faults, and giving instruction for right living.*
                              2 Timothy 3:16 TEV

A NATIONAL CHAMPION IN THE HONESTY BEE

Rosalie Elliott had made it to the fourth round of a national spelling contest in Washington D.C. The eleven-year-old from South Carolina had been asked to spell the word *avowal*. In her soft southern accent she spelled the word, but the judges were not able to determine if she had used an *a* or an *e* as the next to last letter. They debated among themselves for several minutes as they listened to tape recording playbacks. The crucial letter, however, was too accent-blurred to decipher.

Finally, the chief judge put the question to the only person who knew the answer—Rosalie. By this time, Rosalie had heard the correct spelling. Still, without hesitation, she replied that she had misspelled the word.

The entire audience stood and applauded, including some fifty news reporters. Even in defeat, she was a victor. Few remember the name of the first-place winner that year, but Rosalie Elliott is often remembered for her decision to tell the truth.

WISDOM

To be wise, you must have reverence for the Lord.

Job 28:28 TEV

If any of you needs wisdom, you should ask God for it. He is generous and enjoys giving to all people, so he will give you wisdom.

James 1:5 NCV

I will instruct you and teach you in the way you should go; I will counsel you and watch over you..

Psalm 32:8

Getting wisdom is the most important thing you can do! And with your wisdom, develop common sense and good judgment.

Proverbs 4:7 TLB

JUST A STONE

Many years ago in South Africa a man sold his farm so that he might spend his days searching for diamonds. He was consumed with dreams of wealth. Yet when he had finally exhausted his resources and his health, he was no closer to his fortune than on the day he sold his farm.

One day, the man who had bought his farm spotted a strange stone in the creek bed. He liked its shape and placed it on his mantelpiece. A visitor noticed the stone and suggested that it might be a diamond. The farmer quietly had the stone analyzed. Sure enough, it was one of the largest and finest diamonds ever found.

Still operating under great secrecy, the farmer searched his creek, gathering similar stones. They were all diamonds. In fact, the farm was covered with outcrops of them. The farm turned out to be one of the richest diamond deposits in the world.

The lessons of wisdom can often be learned in the relationships and experiences we encounter every day. Ask God to reveal to you what you need to know in order to live the life He desires for you. Very often the resources you need and desire are right in front of you.

WISDOM

I guide you in the way of wisdom and lead you along straight paths. When you walk, your steps will not be hampered; when you run, you will not stumble.

Proverbs 4:11–12

The Lord grants wisdom! His every word is a treasure of knowledge and understanding.

Proverbs 2:6 TLB

Your commands make me wiser than my enemies, because they are mine forever. I am wiser than all my teachers, because I think about your rules.

Psalms 119:98–99 NCV

What seems to be God's foolishness is wiser than human wisdom, and what seems to be God's weakness is stronger than human strength.

1 Corinthians 1:25 TEV

MARKING THE TROUBLE SPOTS

Sara Orne Jewett has written a beautiful novel about Maine, *The Country of the Pointed Firs*. In it, she describes the path that leads a woman writer from her home to that of a retired sea captain named Elijah Tilley. On the way, there are a number of wooden stakes in the ground that appear to be randomly scattered on his property. Each is painted white and trimmed in yellow, just like the captain's house.

Once she arrives at the captain's abode, the writer asks him what the stakes mean. He tells her that when he first made the transition from sailing the seas to plowing the land, he discovered his plow would catch on many of the large rocks just beneath the surface of the ground. Recalling how buoys in the sea always marked trouble spots for him, he set out the stakes as "land buoys" to mark the rocks. Then he could avoid plowing over them in the future.

God's commandments are like buoys for us, revealing the trouble spots and rocky points of life. When we follow God's wisdom and steer clear of what is harmful to us, life is not only more enjoyable, but more productive.

215

WITNESS

"You are *My witnesses,"* says the L*ORD*, *"And
My servant whom I have chosen, That you
may know and believe Me, And understand that
I am He. Before Me there was no God formed,
Nor shall there be after Me."*

Isaiah 43:10 NKJV

*He said to them, "Go into all the world and
preach the gospel to every creature."*

Mark 16:15 NKJV

*"Repentance for forgiveness of sins should be
proclaimed in His name to all the nations,
beginning from Jerusalem."*

Luke 24:47 NASB

*They that were scattered abroad went every
where preaching the word.*

Acts 8:4 KJV

SING HIS PRAISE

Voltaire said that he would destroy, within just a few years, what it took Christ eighteen centuries to establish. He hoped to replace what he perceived as a faulty philosophy with a better one of his own creation. However, Voltaire's words were to become only hollow bragging. His own printing press was later used to print Bibles, and his log cabin became a storage place for them.

Reformation leader Martin Luther once said, "I pray you leave my name alone. Do not call yourselves Lutherans, but Christians." John Wesley expressed a similar sentiment when he said, "I wish the name Methodist might never be mentioned again, but lost in eternal oblivion." Charles Spurgeon said, "I look forward with pleasure to the day when there will not be a Baptist living. I say of the Baptist name, let it perish, but let Christ's own name last forever."

We err anytime we seek to sing our own praises. For the Christian, the only One truly worthy to be praised is the Lord God. Rather than exalt yourself today, seek to exalt the One whose name will last forever, and before whom every knee will one day bow. Let your witness for the Lord ring clear and true, unencumbered by any name but His.

WORK

Even when we were with you, we gave you this rule: "If a man will not work, he shall not eat."
2 Thessalonians 3:10

When God gives any man wealth and possessions, and enables him to enjoy them, to accept his lot and be happy in his work—this is a gift of God.
Ecclesiastes 5:19

Work hard and cheerfully at all you do, just as though you were working for the Lord and not merely for your masters, remembering that it is the Lord Christ who is going to pay you, giving you your full portion of all he owns. He is the one you are really working for.
Colossians 3:23-24 TLB

"Do not work for food that spoils, but for food that endures to eternal life, which the Son of Man will give you."
John 6:27

SELF-SERVE

One day, a grandfather told his grandchildren about his journey to America. He told of being processed at Ellis Island and how he had gone to a cafeteria in lower Manhattan to get something to eat. There, he sat down at an empty table and waited quite some time for someone to take his order. Nobody came. Finally, a woman with a tray full of food sat down opposite him and explained to him how a cafeteria works.

She said, "You start at that end"—pointing toward a stack of trays—"and then go along the food line and pick out what you want. At the other end, they'll tell you how much you have to pay."

The grandfather reflected a moment and then said, "I soon learned that's how everything works in America. Life's a cafeteria here. You can get anything you want—even great success—if you are willing to pay the price. But you'll never get what you want if you wait for someone to bring it to you. You have to get up and get it yourself."

The difference between where you are and where you want to be can often be summed up in one word: work.

WORRY

Don't worry about anything; instead, pray about everything; tell God your needs and don't forget to thank him for his answers.

Philippians 4:6 TLB

"Do not worry about tomorrow; it will have enough worries of its own. There is no need to add to the troubles each day brings."

Matthew 6:34 TEV

Give all your worries and cares to God, for he cares about what happens to you.

1 Peter 5:7 NLT

You will keep him *in perfect peace,* Whose *mind is stayed* on You, *Because he trusts in You.*

Isaiah 26:3 NKJV

A BOX OF MANURE

A story is told of identical twins. One was a hope-filled optimist who often said, "Everything is coming up roses!" The other twin was a sad and hopeless worrier who continually expected the worst to happen. The parents of the twins brought them to a psychologist in hopes that he might be able to bring some balance to their personalities.

The psychologist suggested that on the twins' next birthday, the parents put them in separate rooms to open their gifts. "Give the worrier the best toys you can afford," the psychologist said, "and give the hopeful child a box of manure." The parents did as he suggested.

When they peeked in on the worrier, they heard him loudly complaining, "I'll bet this toy will break. What will happen if I don't like to play this game? There are so many pieces; this toy won't last long because the pieces will all get lost."

Tiptoeing across the corridor, the parents saw their hopeful son gleefully throwing manure up in the air. He laughingly kept saying, "You can't fool me! Where there's this much manure, there has to be a pony!"

How are you looking at life today—as an accident waiting to happen or a blessing about to be received?

WORRY

"The ones on whom seed was sown among the thorns; these are the ones who have heard the word, and the worries of the world, and the deceitfulness of riches, and the desires for other things enter in and choke the word, and it becomes unfruitful."

Mark 4:18-19 NASB

"You cannot add any time to your life by worrying about it."

Matthew 6:27 NCV

Have I not commanded you? Be strong and courageous! Do not tremble or be dismayed, for the LORD your God is with you wherever you go!

Joshua 1:9 NASB

"Peace I leave with you; my peace I give you. I do not give to you as the world gives. Do not let your hearts be troubled and do not be afraid."

John 14:27

RUN TO WIN

In 1987, Eamon Coughlan ran a qualifying heat at the world Indoor Track Championships in Indianapolis. The Irishman was the reigning world record holder at 1500 meters and was favored to win the race. Unfortunately, with two-and-a-half laps left to run, he tripped and fell hard. Even so, Coughlan got up and, with great effort, managed to catch the race leaders. With twenty yards to go, he was in third place, a good enough position to qualify for the final heat.

For some reason Coughlan looked over his shoulder to the inside. Seeing no one in his line of sight, Coughlan relaxed his effort slightly. What he hadn't noticed, however, was that a runner was charging hard on the outside. This runner passed him just a yard from the finish line and eliminated Coughlan from the finals. Worried about his would-be competitors, he had momentarily taken his eyes off the finish line.

You will never reach your goals in life if you allow yourself to be distracted by worry. Make sure your focus is single-minded, and run your race to win!

GOD'S Little Lessons for Teens

Additional copies of this book and other
titles from Honor Books
are available from your local bookstore.

God's Little Lessons on Life
God's Little Lessons on Life for Dad
God's Little Lessons on Life for Graduates
God's Little Lessons on Life for Mom
God's Little Lessons for Teachers
God's Little Lessons for Parents
God's Little Lessons for Leaders

If you have enjoyed this book, or if it has
impacted your life,
we would like to hear from you.

Please contact us at:

Honor Books
Department E
P.O. Box 55388
Tulsa, Oklahoma 74155
Or by e-mail at info@honorbooks.com

HONOR
B O O K S